MW00474831

This book is a true story. A book anyone can read. It is funny at times, sad, and heart wrenching. I could not put it down! And that is a big deal for me because I am not really a person who reads a lot! This book is also written in such a way that it sucks you in and it makes you feel as if you are almost there experiencing parts of it yourself. I cannot wait for the next one!! Amazon Customer

A very heart wrenching story. I cried for her loss. This is a book that everyone should read, as I am sure all of us have taken the wrong path(s) in our life. Janet has such courage to share her deepest despair, and I know sharing has helped her to heal. Her joy with her life is evident by her positive attitude. She gave of herself to help others. S. Gallion

I have only read a few chapters but so far it's a very good book. I can so relate to several things in Janet's life. I also bought one for my daughter. I know she will enjoy reading it as much as I have. Mary

It really should come with a box of tissues, but it doesn't so add it to your cart. Very touching story and one that way too many can relate to. If you've ever made a decision at a young age that affected your whole life, this is a book for you. Peter M.

I was so touched by this book. I realized how deep pain and sorrows of life can just continue, how that it's like an infection that continues to spread. I know the Lord is the only one that can totally heal even to the core of our whole being. Great job, Janet. Thanks for sharing your story. Amazon Customer

This book was Great. Shows how life can be so hard and you can still come through it. Loved the book. Brenda

A story that all need to read. BJEM

I received this book on Thursday and I was finished reading it on Saturday night! This book has everything!! Love, loss, betrayal and faith! Lisa

I can identify with Janet's sorrows about surviving the loss of children so badly desired. It is exactly what I felt during this tough time in my life. The author was very honest and forthcoming in her story. I liked her style of writing. I enjoyed the book very much and recommend it to others. Kindle Customer

Excellent read. The storyteller tells of her difficult teen years and the choices made in these precious years which led her down a road of struggles throughout her life. She does become a Christian as an adult, and God now leads her daily. She still has struggles and challenges, but God is with her as she presses on. C. Williamson

The author pulled me in from the start. Hard to put down. Tears, laughter and a lot of bravery on her part. It is a true story that everyone can relate to. I highly recommend it. Amazon Customer

What a wonderful story! I both laughed and cried. Most importantly, I made connections at many levels to my own life. Thank you, Janet, for sharing your story! N. Lam

Good book. Praise be to our Lord for the changes within us He can make. BLS

I enjoyed your book very much. It touched me in many ways, at times my heart broke for you and at other times you came across as a spoiled brat but overall it shows that you were forced to grow up much quicker than you should have. You as a child had to deal with adult issues which of course was not fair to you. It left me wanting to know more so I am looking forward to your next book. I. Dudley

I read your book. WOW! I was disturbed about many things and I am sorry that as a believer I did not see your pain when you were so young. I had no idea how unhappy you were in Virginia. Your story is truly a story of great pain and triumphant and how the love of God can heal the deepest wounds. I so admire you for your transparency. I pray your book reaches many people. L. Smith

I loved your book!! It was a wonderful testimony. I had no idea you had all those struggles in your life - but now that I just said struggles, it came to me that they were actually blessings in disguise because they made you the wonderful person you are today!!! As we all know, God will use our circumstances in ways to bless us if we just love him and make Him our Lord & Savior- your amazing faith inspires me so-o-o much!! I love you, Janet!! D. Morgan

I just finished, and I absolutely loved it. A. Lamb

This is a *sad* story.
This is a *love* story.
This is a *real* story.
This is ...

<u>MY STORY</u>

-

A young girl's struggle to overcome her past
because of decisions made on her behalf without
consulting her and the consequences that
remained for a lifetime.

Author: Janet Molton Nicholson

This book is based solely on my perceptions and memory **_ONLY!_** Other individuals may remember things differently, but this is precisely why God made us all unique individuals. As Beth Moore stated in her book *So Long, Insecurity, "Each heart knows its own bitterness". (Proverbs 14:10).*

Though it will seem that the majority of this book is about my trial as a young girl and the consequences I suffered from a particular decision made for me, without consulting me, it goes much further than the actual incident … much deeper! The events leading up to this life-changing event, and what occurred afterwards, are just as important as the physical trial itself. I sincerely pray the Lord will guide me in this endeavor and bring things to my remembrance as needed. Though I am the only one who suffered the physical aspects of this situation, I am not the only one affected by it emotionally or mentally. I can try to help you perceive the effect it had on others; however, as for me, I know firsthand what damage it caused in my life. Regardless, make no mistake that it did in fact alter the lives of others.

I procrastinated writing this book. Even as I completed the first draft, I simply laid it aside. I was not sure I wanted to re-live and rehash that period of my life. *Would it even be worth it to put myself through the torment and agony? Would it truly be to anyone's benefit?* I had the mentality that, *"Great … my book is done! I have relived it and now I can just let it go".* It proved to not be as simplistic as healing and moving on. It was more than therapy. I sensed God allowed it all to play out for His benefit and He had a reason for me to tell it to the world. This was all I needed to know. I have forgiven myself and others. I can now share my story knowing that it is for His glory and it will serve whatever purpose He intended. This was all I needed to press forward.

During my much-needed soul searching, I also realized I needed to seek forgiveness from others. Forgiving those I blamed for so much was my main focal point with this book. Though the individuals I sought forgiveness from are no longer able to read the book, I know in my heart they hear my cries for their forgiveness. God showed me I needed to seek forgiveness. I needed to put words to my pain. I hope I have done God justice.

Before I begin, please let me share one last thing. While you are reading this book, whenever I use the words "family member", please keep in mind this does not necessarily refer only to my immediate family (i.e. children, siblings, parents), but it could be a cousin ... a niece ... a nephew ... an uncle ... an aunt. I have made the mistake many times in life **assuming** I knew what I did not know, and I hope you will not make the same mistake. It is not about 'who' but it is about 'what and why'.

It is my greatest desire that you will read and share this book with others! Share it with others! It is a true story. I lived it and I paid a terrible price for the choices I made afterwards! I hope I can prevent the same for someone else.

Chapter One

All young girls … or any child for that matter … look forward to the day they turn 13! On that day, they feel as if they have crossed over from being a child to becoming a teenager. It is a day of liberation. Like most others, I have thought about my BIG DAY for quite some time. The opportunity to tell people I was a teenager could not come fast enough. I would be in junior high school and I knew it would be everything I anticipated it would be. I had dreamed of this day for so long.

We can stop many things in life, but time is the one thing we have no control over. We cannot change or alter time no matter how strong the desire. Time finally brought me my big day, and I was ready to embrace it.

However, this birthday would not be the highly anticipated day I had dreamed of for many years. I would not have the celebration with gifts and balloons, along with a house full of family and friends. Rather I would find myself basically alone and very downtrodden. The many friends I had for most of my life would not be coming to my house to help me celebrate. There would be no birthday streamers hanging across the ceiling. There would be no balloons of multiple colors swaying throughout the room. I would hear no music coming from the record player and I would not see the table laden with food.

I would not wake on this morning with butterflies in my stomach or the heightened emotion of anticipation. I would not see my new party dress hanging from the closet door waiting for me to put on. I was not twirling around in my bedroom excitedly thinking of the moment when I would enter the room and share this special day with friends and family. There would be no cake. The party I had envisioned would not happen. In the place of excitement and cheer, there would be much anger and disillusionment. I would be battling a huge change in my life and it would not be a welcomed one.

I was born the first child of my parent's marriage. Though I was their oldest child, I was not the eldest child in our family. When my parents married, you had *"his children, her children, and our children"*. This alone would cause many obstacles in life but that is yet another book for another time. Having three sets of children was not the ideal way to start a new marriage. It had quite the impact on my life, as I am sure it did on all of us. I can only speak for myself but having this blended family would prove to be very difficult for me at times. How we are raised, the things we endure during childhood, the statements made to us, the incidents we witness, all these things tend to mold us into the person we become. Many circumstances and people brought me to this place in life and played a key role in who I am today.

I was born on December 10, 1957, in Baltimore, Maryland. From stories I have heard and things that have been said, I know my parents were not head over heels in love when they married. When they met, they were both at crossroads in their lives where they had no choice but to focus more on circumstance than on romance. They found solace in each other and a resting place they both so needed at this stage in their lives. In sharing this, I must tell you that what I am stating here is what has been told to me growing up. I do not know this firsthand and there are many out there who will find pleasure in contradicting what I share. I chose to believe my parents' story over what others would want me to believe.

When my parents met, my mom was a single parent, trying to raise two sons. She worked at a small coffee house as a waitress. My dad was in the middle of a divorce, and he was the father of four daughters and a son. Whether my mom was divorced or not, I do not know.

From things I have heard and learned over the years, my dad's first marriage was not a good one. However, I would like you to know that throughout the course of my life, I had opportunity on more than one occasion to meet my dad's ex-wife. She was a very nice person to me and I only have fond memories of her. I do not know the circumstances of their divorce, but I was left to believe there was a lot of animosity, pain, and unforgiveness by all involved. Divorce is a horrendous ordeal for children to have to endure. No matter how easy the parents try to make it on the children, it leaves scars which sometimes never heal. When you have a messy situation, as I have heard this was, then the turmoil and destruction it renders is life changing. Some scars never heal or go away in the lives of the children. No one wins in divorce and always it is the children that lose the most.

As for my mom's first marriage, I understand it was not bad. It was just minus the husband more times than not. They were young, and a lack of maturity played a huge part in the demise of this marriage. I also understood my grandmother was a large obstacle in this union as she was controlling over my mom and my mom's life. Ironically, it would be my mom's ex-husband who would share this with me as I would get an opportunity later in life to meet him and spend time with him. We became very good friends and spent time together. I came to know him as a special person and I was very fond of him. Years later, as a grown woman and after he had passed away, I would get the opportunity to meet his extended family, and we would all become friends. They are all wonderful and caring individuals. I am only sad we could not have bonded earlier in life. I think it would have enhanced the lives of my older brothers and enriched their lives in a positive manner.

As I stated earlier, when my parents met, mom was working as a waitress trying to put food on the table and keep a roof over the heads of herself and her two young sons. I had the impression she received no monetary assistance from her ex-husband. I do not know the whole story or even if this is true. I caution you not to jump to conclusions where there are no facts to render. We need to keep in mind that there are three sides to every story … *his side, her side, and the truth!* I do know when I met my mom's ex-husband he had a family he supported, and he seemed to be stable in life. Knowing this, I can only assume that youth played a huge part in his absence in the lives of my brothers. It does not justify it, but I do not think any of us can say we never made mistakes which did not affect others. I just ask you to refrain from passing judgment throughout the course of this book on anyone. It simply was what it was, and we all move on. As adults we are responsible for whether we choose to continue reveling in the past or whether we mature and move forward. I pray for all intents and purposes that my readers choose to look ahead and not back. Unforgiveness and **my refusal** to accept things as they were has caused me and others more years of hardship than I care to remember. History will not change based on our feelings. We all need to accept history as it was, learn from it, and be of a healthy mind in our future.

From the onset, my parent's union would be riddled with major problems. Mom and Dad found enough of whatever it was they needed in each other and they married. *Was it the right decision?* During the early years of their marriage, I am sure they would have answered 'no' to that question. But based on their last fifteen or so years together, I would hear my mom say on more than one occasion how she would relive every moment again if she knew the ending would be as it was. She and my dad had reached a place in their lives where they were totally in love and truly became one. Knowing this, I would have to say 'yes', it was the right decision for them at that time. They would deal with all the ensuing issues which arose out of this marriage and come to know a love unlike any other. They were blessed with 49 years of marriage before mom would go home to be with the Lord. (*Note: During my mom's funeral, it was brought to my attention there was no way my parents could have been married for 49 years. Again, I do not know for sure and I really do not care. They were together, and they loved one another … end of story!*)

As I watched my parents in their later years it amazed me how they truly took on a child-like love for one another. Their hearts were one. They sought to put each other above all else. It is those later years I will always remember and hold dear in my heart.

Many years after the passing of my mom, Dad was in the early stages of Alzheimer's. Once the dust had settled and the realization that mom was not returning home became apparent, Dad became very obsessive with visiting her at the cemetery. His first words each morning were, *"Who is taking me to see Mom today?"* And, his last words at night were, *"Who is taking me to see Mom tomorrow?"* We had numerous caregivers with daddy while he was able to reside at home. They would literally pack lunches to take my dad to visit Mom. They took chairs and spent time at the head of her grave. I have many pictures of daddy decorating Mom's grave for New Year's, her January birthday, Valentine's Day, St. Patrick's

Day, Easter, Mother's Day, Fall, Spring, Summer, Thanksgiving, and Christmas. He made sure she was not forgotten. It was only as his Alzheimer's progressed that he started to forget, and days would pass between visits. It was both heart wrenching and heartwarming!!!

Chapter Two

My earliest memories are of our family living in the community of Berkshire, not far from Dundalk, in the State of Maryland. Prior to that time, I only have bits and pieces of memories ... *flashbacks really* ... but nothing concrete. I cannot even say if they are memories, or if they were stories embedded in my mind by things I heard over the years. I know of family who have shared with me that they have lost remembrance of years in their life also. It has often puzzled us. It has caused me to wonder if what I remember was actually fact or fiction. I truly believe we can hear the same story over and over during our growing years ... see pictures that match these stories ... and we can get to the point where we truly believe these are our memories. *But are they really, or are they what we were told?*

My years in Berkshire were awesome years for me. Up until we relocated, I was the average child from the average home. Basically, I remember being a happy child. I thought we were just like all the other families. We had the swimming pool in the backyard. I had the nice clothes to wear to school. I was involved in all sorts of activities. As far as I was concerned, I thought I had it all. My mom was very involved in my school and was a social butterfly. She even wrote a column called the "Berkshire Beat" which was published in the weekly newspaper.

My mom was a 'hands on' mom, and she was very active in my life. Each week I bowled, and I played softball. I took tap and ballet lessons. I took roller skating lessons and was also learning to play the organ. My mom coached a softball team. I could not play on her team since I was her daughter, so I played on an opposing team. My mom also played on a young adult league for herself. For all intents and purposes, I was a happy little girl. I had the pet dog, the pet cat, and we even had a parrot at one time. Could life be any more perfect?

Everyone knew my mom and referred to her as "Mom Molton". Our home was where everyone congregated on the weekends. Nothing made my mom happier than to have her children's friends come to her house. Today I am the same way. Nothing makes this mom's heart shine more than to have her children's friends come and spend time at our home. As you can see, I get it naturally.

My dad, on the other hand, was a different story. He was a workaholic and drank quite a bit. He was away from home a lot, and I can remember at one time in my life where he worked three jobs. When he ate and slept was beyond me. Somehow, he must have managed to find time for his family because I can remember him and my mom working on Friday and Saturday nights at the school … hosting a Preteen and Teen Center. They had a dance every weekend for the youth, and they were both in attendance. My parents went to dances and sometimes got together with the neighbors to play cards. They had friends and a social circle they were active in. They were both on the PTA at school. I was blessed in a lot of ways.

As a child, I do not remember many times that we, as a family, ever sat down for a meal without a strange face at the dinner table. At times, we really did look like the Waltons. My dad made a wooden dinner table for us to use because we could not afford to buy one to accommodate our needs. When we moved from our location, dad had to saw the table into thirds to get it out of the house. True story … I promise! I love sharing this part of my life as it makes me feel warm and fuzzy inside.

There were difficult times thrown in the mix, but I have more good memories than bad.

I think my dad's main objective in life was to give us the best he could, and he did. I know he carried a great burden in his heart for the distance between him and his children from his first marriage. My dad did not talk a lot about his past or unpleasant things. It was easier for him to just keep things inside and deal with them on his own. There were times when he would speak of his other children and you could see the longing and sadness in his eyes. He never got to be the dad to them I felt he wanted to be. His absence in their lives caused a lot of misconceptions on the part of many, but I know my dad loved all his children dearly.

In the eyes of a young girl, my dad was my hero and I was his little princess. Many times, I would hear the story of how my dad carried a colored picture of me, at the age of two or three, in his wallet. I love hearing the story of the time my dad was in a bar with some pals. He was showing this picture off to anyone in the bar who appeared interested and would listen to his story. I do not know the details of the story he would tell, but dad would share this picture with any eyes willing to look. At some point during the storytelling, another bar patron would call him a liar and say the picture was that of a baby doll. Of course, as I was told, the typical barroom brawl erupted. How it ended, I do not know. All I knew was my dad was my protector, my provider, and he could do no wrong in my eyes. Did this mean he did no wrong? No, but does anyone live a completely good life? I say not! But in the eyes of his princess, nothing he did was wrong. I would be told repeatedly over the years how I was the apple of his eye.

Though I loved hearing over and over how much I meant to my daddy, I know in my heart my dad loved all of us in his own very special way.

A few years ago, I discovered something which might have devastated my life, but I have since come to grips with the reality of it all. At the time, it made me wonder if this was why daddy was so protective of me. *Was he scared I would discover this secret and not love him anymore? Did he think I would disown him and Mom?* I do not know, but it did not change my love for either of them. It left me with a lot of questions, but I have since come to the realization that I will never have answers to those questions.

I just lied to you! The part above where I indicated I came to grips with the secret I discovered was a big fat lie! As much as I tried to fool myself and tell myself that what I discovered was not important to me, it turned out it truly was. I finally reached out to the only person left who could tell me anything to help me lay this all to rest.

Before reaching out to the one person who might be able to shed some light on this situation for me, I struggled internally for years. I lied to myself daily and to others by saying it simply did not matter. I was convincing. *Is this not what we do in life ... we deceive others, but we deceive ourselves even more?* We are not good at being honest with ourselves. You would think if you could be truthful with anyone in the world, it would be with oneself. The Bible speaks of our deceptive hearts. In Jeremiah 17:9 it states, *"The heart is deceitful above all things, and desperately wicked; who can know it?"* Our hearts are the central part of our being. In our thoughts, feelings, and actions, our hearts deceive us daily. This is why it is so important not to make rash decisions based on emotion. *What controls our emotions ... our HEART!!!*

At the time this occurred, I was working for a law firm in Charlottesville, Virginia, and I had been walking with the Lord for about seven or eight years. I wish I could tell you I was a 'mature' Christian, but in many ways, I was not. I thought I was but in looking back I cannot deny that I had a lot of growth still needed in my Christian walk. I could claim maturity in many ways in that I no longer frequented the bars. I did not surround myself with the partiers from my past. I was a dedicated mother. Emotions, however, were a completely different ballgame. As mature as I was on one hand, I was very immature on the other. I still allowed my emotions to rule over me. I could not handle stress. I could not handle fear. I could not handle any upheaval in my otherwise Christian existence. I had many struggles during this time, and when something was amiss in my life which effected my emotions, I fell to pieces. I would miss work because I was so emotionally distraught I could not function. I had faith in God, but I did not know how to walk out that faith. I would lose positions of employment simply because I was immature in my emotions.

When looking at my life, it would appear I was very happy during these early years. Alcohol, however, would be a detriment to my otherwise happy existence. It seemed to be everywhere. Behind closed doors, my parents dealt with a great deal and it caused friction in our home.

I guess if we were at all honest with ourselves, there is no such thing as a perfect life as a child. You may not have experienced some of the things I call traumatic for me, but on the flip side, I did not experience the horrible things other children endure in life. I just know we all have skeletons in our closets we hope never come out. We choose to remember either the good or the bad. I have made a conscious decision to focus on the positive. In comparison to the negative, I have to say there were more positives. I did not always agree with this. For many years, I wallowed in the negative because I thought it was to my benefit to do so. If we choose to focus only on the negative, then it seems to justify all the wrong we do. It becomes our excuse for everything and we get absorbed in the blame game.

Somewhere in time, I came to feel personally responsible for my family. I am not sure what transpired to make such a young person take on this burden. I have searched my mind over and over throughout the years in an effort to understand how this could have come about. I keep returning to a scene from my grandmother's funeral which I sense sealed this fate in my life. I was sitting on a chair in the funeral home. As you can imagine, my mother was very distraught over the death of her mother. I was only about 10 years of age. I was sitting there crying. I do not know whether I was crying for my mother or for my grandmother. I would have to guess for my mother since I do not have many memories of my grandmother. A family member came up to me and said, *"Janet Leigh, you have to stop crying. Your mother needs you to be strong for her."* I guess I took those words to heart and they became a path I still travel somewhat to this very day. Though I have, through the grace of God, learned to set certain boundaries in my life, I still have not completely given up this role. For most of my childhood and straight into my adult life, I had to be strong ... not just for Mom but for my entire family.

I feel responsible at times for all my family members. Again, this is a burden I do not carry as often as I did, but there were times in my life when I went over and above to protect my family. But as you will discover as you reach farther into my story, I looked at my siblings not only as my sisters and brothers, but as my children in a sense. I know you may not understand this completely, but when you are placed in the role of caretaker then you take on a different identity and you relate to those you are caring for in a different way. I just came to this realization a short time ago. I always wondered why I took it so personally when something bad happened to a family member, more so a sibling. It is because they played a bigger role in my life than they should have. Yes, we all care tremendously for our siblings, but it was more than that for me. I played a huge part in their early years even though they do not remember this. It gave me a bigger sense of responsibility for them.

What I perceived as a sense of responsibility for family, in the eyes of some ... especially as they became adults ... they perceived as me being bossy and controlling. I sincerely felt resentment from them. I have learned through counseling that I was not meaning to be bossy and controlling, but I had such a deep passion for the welfare of my family. Today I still feel resentment from some when I interject my emotion of preferring they not do this or that. I had one family member simply tell me it was none of my business and they were a grown adult. I heard what they said ... what they said was more than true ... but I was only offering what I did out of love and concern and not out of a need to be in control. I struggle daily with simply keeping my mouth shut and praying.

To this very day, when I know one of my family members is suffering in any way, I take on this sense of *"I have to do something"*. It truly is very deeply ingrained in me. I can feel this fear in me rising at the prospect of anyone I love being in difficult situations. Just typing this and thinking of my loved ones in trouble or suffering brings tears to my eyes. I know none of them have ever understood the depth of my feeling responsible for their well-being. How could they even begin to contemplate how this affects me, when I do not even know the true meaning of how this came to be? I take it personally is all I know. It has caused me so much heartache and loss in my own personal life. My family is not responsible for the hardships I have brought on myself trying to protect them or help them out of a situation. They have not required this of me or made me feel like I had a personal responsibility to them. It had to be something that originated when I was young, but for now, I have no one thing I can point at and say this is what caused me to be this way.

Being the caretaker robbed me of so much of my own young life. It would take me years to work through the bitterness this left in me. Heck, it would take me years to even realize I had bitterness. Praise God, He brought me to it and He brought me through it.

Because I took on this maternal role at such an early age, I feel my family fed into it, whether intentional or not. There were times when I felt I had to resolve whatever issues were causing their pain. I literally could have gone to jail at one time in my life for something I did to help a family member. They never knew the extent I went to in order to help them, but that personal responsibility I felt led me to do what I did. I know for a fact that this family member would never ever have jeopardized my well-being for anything. Had they known what I had to do to assist them, I know they would have been devastated. I am sure had it ever come to light I would have been judged harshly by society. No one wants to look at the *why's* in people's lives … they only want to see what they think they know.

On another note, family members made me feel responsible for certain situations at times. I know they never meant to do this, but I guess once I acclimated myself to the caretaker role, they could not help but be led to do the same. There would be many times in my young life and adult life where I risked my very own freedom … *my very own marriage … my very own sense of well-being* … in order to provide for them.

As a result of feeling personally responsible for my family, I knew I could not let my parents down, especially my dad. My dad and mom expected much of me. I knew this, and it steered the course of my life for many, many years. It would be a concept I accepted from a very young age until I was a grown woman with children and grandchildren. Bottom line, I felt personally responsible for the care and well-being of my family … *all of them* … from my parents to my older siblings and right down to the younger ones.

Despite all of this, my life in Maryland was good whether with discord from time to time or not. Dad and mom had big dreams for their little girl. Up until this point, I was moving along according to their plans and enjoying every minute of it. I was into everything possible. I was popular and had lots of friends. My mom and I had so many mother/daughter events we did together. I felt very close to her. I did not see what was waiting ahead for me, so when it came, it literally turned my world upside down.

Chapter Three

The day would come when my parents would make the decision that it was in our family's best interest to leave our home in Maryland. My dad was getting ready to retire from Bethlehem Steel after thirty years of service. My parents were at a crossroads. It was time to decide whether to move back to my dad's hometown of South Fork, Pennsylvania, or my mom's hometown of Louisa, Virginia. Life was beginning to move too fast in the city. It was taking its toll on my family in many ways and touching the lives of us all.

Unbeknownst to my parents and though I was a very happy little girl, life in the city was affecting me also. I was partying at all hours of the night with friends, drinking and having fun. It was easy for me to sneak out of the house. My parents were so focused on other issues, both in their marriage and in our family, that they did not notice what was happening in my life. I did well in school. On the surface, I was a good girl.

My friends were already having sex, but for some reason, I never ventured quite that far. I even had girlfriends that were personally involved with one or more of my family members. Despite what I was doing, there were family members who were very protective of me and our inner circles did cross. They were very aware of my drinking and partying, but it was a norm for kids at that time. They had their own battles in life so my doing what I did was accepted. Because of the fact we knew so many of the same people, I was very careful about certain things. My drinking alcohol and partying was acceptable to them. It was almost expected, but when it came to drugs, there lay a completely different story. Their experimenting with drugs was one thing, but they did not want drugs in my life.

I remember being at a party in the basement of a friend's house. Everyone there was standing around in a circle, drinking and having fun. Someone passed a marijuana joint to me. I had never tried drugs of any sort, so I thought, *'what the heck'*. As I put the joint to my mouth, out of nowhere I felt this slap across my face. A family member had walked in at that precise moment, and they were not happy with what I was getting ready to do. Never mind this was something they did on a daily basis. It simply was not something I would be allowed to do, and it was made very clear to everyone.

Our lives were spiraling out of control and we were a train wreck waiting to happen. As time would have it, we wrecked eventually in more ways than one. The dysfunction in our family was getting worse by the day, and no one had the energy … *the know-how … the inclination … the tools …* or the knowledge to stop it.

Living in Maryland, drugs and alcohol were becoming more prevalent daily in lives all around us and it was becoming more than my parents could handle. They had enough to deal with in their own personal lives. Instead of facing situations head on, we left. Leaving and avoiding real life issues would become a routine in my life. It was always easier than the alternative.

I had already been to the funeral of one friend due to an overdose of drugs. I can remember how devastated his family was. I watched as his girlfriend … my friend … struggled to understand all of this. I think this episode in my life is what prevented me from being a drug user in the future. As I became older, I would dapple in drugs here and there but nothing which took root. I probably only did it to appear cool and feel like a part of the gang. How sad is that? I loved my alcohol, but I was always very afraid to do drugs. I guess this was a blessing in some ways. However, be it alcohol or drugs, an addiction is still the same and the long-range repercussions are not worth the temporary pleasure.

Some within my family unit, immediate and extended, were experimenting with heavy drugs and my parents were fearful at how fast these substances were seeping into our lives. Never mind the fact that alcohol was already wrecking havoc in our family. However, for whatever reason, drinking was not seen as a problem. It was a norm in those days, as it is today. It was the least of our problems. Only what was coming into our lives from the outside world was perceived as a problem. Life moves fast in the big cities. Look at what I was already introduced to at the age of 10 and 11.

Much later in life, as I was raising my daughter, I would look at her sometimes and compare our lives at the same age. The idea of her even contemplating the things I did at such an early age was out of the question. She was playing with Cabbage Patch dolls. To my knowledge, she did not even have a concept about alcohol or drugs.

There was always friction between my parents for one reason or another. My mom was forever protecting "her" children from what was perceived as my dad's wrath. It was not that my dad was a bad person by any means. He was, however, very strict. Also, at times, I think he was hard on my brothers because of the inner turmoil he had daily within himself over the fact that his son from his first marriage was not with him. I think jealously caused a lot of the issues between dad and family. Of course, my dad's drinking was causing a great deal of the friction, but we would never acknowledge this. There was lack of communication in our home. There was always hollering and screaming. We did not know how to discuss things rationally in an effort to work things out. Everything was a battle. I am surprised we were ever able to resolve anything. *Or did anything ever get resolved?* I think most problems were shoved under the rug and never really dealt with.

My parents did make one decision and it was one that changed the course of all our lives. They decided we would move to Virginia … to the country … to a place that had to be better than where we lived. By this time, my dad was a few months short of his retirement, so the wheels were put into motion and the move was imminent. My mom would take the children and go to Virginia. My dad would join us later.

We also would be making this move minus one family member who was already married. I do not know how old that person was, but I am sure they were in their late teens. There was no big church wedding. It was the kind of service that was held quietly because of the circumstances. A baby was on the way, and this was frowned on back in the late 60's. According to what I overheard, this was not an everyday occurrence. *Or maybe it was, and it just wasn't for us.* I do know, however, in those days, they did not have the legal options that women have today. (*Note: I would like to say that this 'circumstance' which encouraged the marriage was an awesome son whom we lost way too early in life. What if they had chosen abortion or some other option to get rid of their son? I praise God and them for their fortitude to press on and allow their son to be born. He brought much joy to so many and touched many* *lives in his short time here. He left behind children, so the legacy lives on. **BUT** what if?)*

To say I was heartbroken about the move would be an understatement. I was twelve years old and I did not want to leave all my friends and the world I grew up in. I wanted to start the 9th grade at Dundalk Senior High School and go on to graduate with my friends. I had a boyfriend (whatever that meant at that age) and his name was Buddy. I did not want to leave him. In my eyes, leaving Maryland and my boyfriend were the worse things my parents could do to me. Pouring even more salt in the wound, we were leaving a family member behind. I felt like my family was breaking up. I would never ever be able to endure this move. My life as I knew it would never be the same. *Seems dramatic, huh?* Well in the mind of a young girl, it was. I was anything but prepared.

There were no family discussions about this move. We did not share our feelings about how we felt. The decision was made for us children, and we had no choice but to go along.

I do not think my parents were really prepared for the hardships this move would have on them either. In Maryland my parents shared a life that was outgoing and fun. Sure, it had difficulties, but it was the life they were accustomed to living. It enabled them to occasionally put their problems and the evils that lurked in our home on the back burner. It was a momentary escape from reality for them. They could laugh and forget the issues that invaded their daily lives. This would not be the case in Virginia. Though my mom had family in Virginia, small towns can be very judgmental and that would eventually bring our house of cards tumbling down. It would rob our family of so much, and it set us on an even greater course of destruction.

Chapter Four

There were issues from the minute we touched down in Virginia. It was another planet to me ... a world totally different from the one I was accustomed to. My parents would never really bond with people as they did in Maryland. This alone would bring hardships in their lives that would wreck havoc of its own. My dad would find a place of acceptance early on in business, but I am not sure my mom ever did, at least not right away. She eventually had girlfriends, but she had left her bestie in Maryland.

To make matters even worse, the activities that were readily available to us in the big city would not be so available to us in the country. Our lives as we knew it would be forever changed and the effects on each of us would take its own toll.

Originally, we made the move without my dad and one other family member. My dad would come home on weekends. He would eventually retire and come home permanently but not in the beginning. This was quite an adjustment for me. I was not used to having dad as a part-time dad. Even though he worked so much where he was hardly ever at home when we were in Maryland, it was difficult to accept he was not with us during the week. I felt like my family was going in all different directions. All these things combined caused me to feel resentment towards my parents for what they were doing to us and to our family. I would say I hated them, but hate is a bit strong. I do not think I could have ever sincerely hated my parents. I was just very unhappy for what they were doing to us. My sense of security was being tampered with and my defenses were going up. It would become a mechanism I would use throughout the course of my young life … *shutting down when things hurt!*

We finally arrived at the home we would rent in Virginia. I simply cannot put in words how I felt. I was not even open to trying to like this set up. *How selfish was that of me?* At my age you were not capable of being open-minded. It was not what I ever had to do before. I was spoiled and very self-centered. I never had to be anything less. In my mind, this move was the most horrible thing a parent could do to a child my age. It simply depleted me and destroyed the safety net that all children should be able to rely upon. I knew I would never adjust. I had so many questions and so few answers. *How could they take us out of a world so full of life and promise, to a world that was simply nothing?* We were in the middle of nowhere. *Where is the Burger King at the end of the street? Where is the bowling alley that is supposed to be in walking distance? Where are the neighbors whose homes were so close we could hear them sneeze? Where are the houses, the sidewalks, the alleys?* All I could think was, "*What in the world are they doing to me?*" It all became about me. I was much too young to worry about anyone else.

I keep saying I was '*too young*' for this and that, but as I write this book, I realize how wrong I am in saying this. It is all about how we are raised. Sure, there is a lot of immaturity at this age in life which plays a factor, but I think we can raise our children in a way where they are more family focused than entirely on self. When you have a family which truly acts as a unit and not separately … when they sit down and discuss family issues as a whole … then I think they have more of a tendency to feel as if the decision was a part of their making. They feel included and not as if they are being made to live out the decisions of others. They become part of the process and it makes them more desirous to work as a team to accomplish the goal at hand. This was not the case for our family. We all were separate individuals working alone the majority of the time. We were all we worried about. We did not know any other way.

Children have a way of taking things which cause their worlds to turn upside down and blaming themselves. Parents get a divorce and we wonder what we did to bring this about. This was how I was feeling. I wondered what I had done that was so terrible we had to uproot our lives and move to Virginia. I thought I was a good child.

Obviously, my siblings and I must have done something so drastic to cause my parents to make such a rash decision without consulting us and seeing how we felt. It had to be my fault. *Did I stay out too late one too many times? Did they find out I was experimenting with alcohol at such an early age and trying marijuana? Was it because I ran away from home with a girlfriend once?* It had to be because of all of this, or they would not have done this to me? It is amazing how it was all about me.

Could it possibly be because they believe I am no longer a virgin? Many of my other friends in Maryland were openly experimenting with sex. Did they not realize I would never hurt them in such a way? I have only kissed one boy. Should I tell them this? Maybe if they think I have had sex and I tell them it is not true, then they will return to Maryland. I could not believe this was happening. It had to be a nightmare I would awaken from soon.

Forget the idea of me talking to my parents about anything. What would I say? My parents and I did not talk about such things. It simply was not proper or the right thing to do. If I said something like this to them, then they would move because obviously if I spoke to them of such things, it would be evident to them that something must be going on. As ignorant as it sounds, this would be the mindset I had for a very long time.

Communication could have prevented all these thoughts from settling within me. A family meeting explaining the whys of all of this could have stopped the negative thinking growing within, but it simply was not the way it was done in our family. Decisions were made. Before we knew it, our worlds were turned upside down. We had no idea why, but we were expected to understand.

According to my way of thinking, my life was forever ruined. I would never see the friends I loved again, and they would be forever left behind. *What about my god-Mother? What would I do without her?* She was my mom's best friend and my safety net. She was my safety net for everything. There was nothing I did not share with her. I went to her when Mom and I would be screaming at one another. She hugged me. She was there for me, and she was now gone too.

Though I loved my parents dearly, I slowly began to despise them for what they did to me. I would not say these things to them because we were raised to be strong. I could not disappoint my parents yet again, as I had obviously done. I had to win their approval back. They have had so many disappointments in life as it is, and I was going to do big things … *remember?* For their sakes, I would keep all these negative feelings inside and I would go with the flow … whatever the flow was going to be.

After acceptance on some level finally set in, I had to wonder to myself "*Now what*"? It would be years before I had a driver's license. You could bet on one thing though ... the minute I had that license in my hands, I would return to Berkshire. I do not belong in Virginia! I would just play along until the day I could return to where I truly felt I was meant to be ... *Maryland!* At my age, I truly did not perceive surviving this upheaval in my life. The other children, except for my older brothers, were younger than me. They would not even remember the move, but this would not be the case with me. *How can my parents not understand this? What in the world are they thinking?*

Chapter Five

We finally settled into our new home. It was the summer of 1970 and I was about as lost as a fish out of water. I had no friends. I had no one to call and chat with. To fill the void I was feeling, I would spend time locked in my bedroom writing letters to my friends back home. I was so homesick, and I knew I simply would never make it here. You would think getting letters from my friends in Maryland would help the situation. It did not. It was only making me more homesick and depressed. I thought it was best to just quit writing, so I did.

Dad and mom purchased a building not far from the home we were renting, and they renovated it into a general store. They spent a great deal of time away from home. Having dad gone was no big deal as that had been the norm for us, but now my mom was away from home also.

Prior to the start of school, Mom did everything in her power to get us excited about going. She would take us over to relative's homes in the hope we would all bond with their children. However, this was probably not a good idea at all. My parents never knew because I never shared this with them ... or with anyone for that matter ... but one of my distant male family members would mess with me sexually when we would travel to Virginia from Maryland to visit. He never forced me to have sex, but it came as close as it could without having committed the act. I was too scared to ever share this with my parents. I did not want anyone to get into trouble. To this day, I have never shared this with anyone, but I never forgot it. It continued for a few months or so and then he stopped. I am not sure why he stopped, but he did. When I see him today as an adult, he acts like nothing ever happened. It makes me sick to my stomach ... just another thing hidden and never revealed. It would be another reason I would feel so alone and insecure in the years to come.

Eventually, in preparation of my big first day at school, I got to buy all new clothes. For a fleeting moment, this helped. Then we returned home, and I again sank back into the pit of depression I seemed to live in during those days.

Up until this time, I thought my mom and I were ok. Sure, we had our ups and downs as most mothers and daughters had, but we did mother-daughter things. Now it was changing rapidly, and we were not getting along well. This situation was not helping. I spent most of my days in my room, daydreaming of the day I could return to Maryland. It was all I thought about.

Mom did not seem to be happy either. I am not sure why, but something just never felt right. I thought this move was for our best. *So, what was wrong?*

Shortly after we settled in Virginia, we did get some good news. The family member who was married was relocating to Virginia also. I was very happy about this, but even so, it was not enough to pull me out of the funk I seemed to stay in.

I lacked motivation to do much of anything. I was still so angry. I realized my parents thought they were doing what was best for us, but how could this be best? We never had family time anymore ... not that we really had any to begin with. We did not have the activities we once had. We did not have the friends in and out of our home as we used to have.

My parents had to be affected by this as well. This was quite a culture shock for them also. Instead of a social life filled with friends and special times, my parents were working all the time trying to make ends meet. I knew they were sad because I could see it. Whenever they were at home together, which was rarely, they seemed to do nothing but argue.

Instead of waking to my mom cooking breakfast, it was I who had the care for my three younger siblings. It was up to me to feed them, bathe them, play with them, and basically be there for them. I was responsible for the upkeep of the home. We seldom had family dinners together because dad was at the store from opening until closing. Mom was depressed a great deal of the time, and she had lost so much of her joy. How could she feel otherwise? Everything they envisioned by making this move was gradually falling through. Though my mom was born and raised one county over, the community we moved to did not seem as accepting of fresh ideas from city folk. My parents tried to get involved with the local PTA as they once were in Maryland, but things were so different here. I heard on more than one occasion how the members of the school's PTA rejected every idea my parents put on the table.

Small towns I think are wonderful and great, but I truly learned that unless you are born to a family within that town and raised within the county, are part of a family with deep roots, or are retiring there with no children, then you are never truly accepted. Of course, if you are rich, then you tend to blend in a bit easier. Unfortunately, we were not any of the things above… not yet!

We strived to make new friends and life seemed to be getting better, but when the chips are down, we soon learned that small-town people cling to their own. This is how I came to feel at a very early age. Unfortunately, it remained with me throughout a lot of my growing years. I cannot say this is true today. I continue to reside in a small town and I have had the privilege of meeting some very caring people. You cannot judge everyone by the stuffiness of some. It simply was what I was feeling at such an early age ... *call it a lack of maturity and a lot of self-centeredness.*

I think my parents felt rejected more than we would ever know. Sure, they made the occasional friendships ... some became very close ... but my dad's drinking intensified over the years, and my mother's need for a life caused her to focus more on her pain then on her social life. She suffered with great bouts of depression. Our family was simply out of control. Each of us was trying to find that place of solace on our own and none of us were able to see outside of ourselves. No, my parents did not neglect us by far. My parents loved their children more than anything or anyone in this world. We were cared for and loved deeply. If I had to pinpoint just one thing my parents were at fault for, it would be they loved us too much and overcompensated for it at times. They were constantly giving to us. Even when they had financial hardships, they seemed to always find a way to keep giving. What a burden it must have been for them. I know finances would always be a conflict. It caused a lot of turmoil.

Now that I am grown and know more about things then I did then, I have to wonder at times if being in Virginia and around certain members of her family caused some of my mother's bouts of depression. I knew my mom had been sexually abused by distant male members of her extended family when she was younger. This had to be difficult and very emotional especially since she was living in close proximity with them.

Eventually my dad's business prospered to the point where we were financially set. What we lacked in attention (and what I perceived as a lack of love) was more than made up for with material things. Nevertheless, something was always missing. I think the lines of communication between my parents, and between parent and child, ceased to exist. We were all wrapped up in our individual anger and disappointment. Being parents did not make them any less susceptible to this pain. Their worlds had been turned upside down, too. At my age, I was not capable of seeing anything beyond me. I only saw and felt my loss and withdrawing was what I learned to do best.

We did have some fun times even though I choose only to remember the bad. Looking back, I remember us playing softball in the field beside the house we rented. It was times like these that seemed far and few between. I cherish those times nonetheless.

Another fond memory I have is of my dad purchasing a tractor. By this time, we had purchased our own home and it was most definitely not a farm. We had no more use for a tractor than a preacher has for the devil! My dad bought it for fun. To us 'city slickers', it was great entertainment to pile the family on that tractor, so dad could ride us up and down the country roads. I chuckle as I type this because I know how hilarious this sounds. To us, it was the greatest thing. My dad was the greatest!!!!

School finally started. I could not forget, however, that this should have been my first day at Dundalk Senior High School in Maryland. I had looked forward to this day for so long. What should have been my coming out year turned into dread. In my little warped mind, the people I had encountered over the summer were not cool like my friends in Berkshire. *They dressed like country folk. They rode horses for crying out loud! Where was the crowd on the corner at night, hiding their beer and smoking cigarettes in secret? Where was the loud music from cars going by? Where were all the boys that hung out at our house with my brothers? Where were all my parents' friends? Who were they going to go to dances with on the weekend or play cards with? Where were all my girlfriends that I could giggle with and share my deepest secrets with? How did they know what turf belonged to who … where we live now, it's all TURF!!! All I saw was turf for miles and miles.* I knew I would never recover from this move. DRAMA, DRAMA, DRAMA~!!!

I had been in school for a few months and I had some real shockers to adjust to. I went from a school with over a thousand students to one that only had hundreds. The activities which I once participated in were no longer available to me. There was no gymnastics team. There was no softball. I could not for the life of me figure out what students did. When we lived in Maryland, we were actively involved in so many things. At one time, I remember my mom had rented a large bus and took a load of teenagers to New York on a field trip. This was what brought her so much joy. She loved doing things like this. She was so involved in our lives. Since relocating to Virginia, we did not seem to have the same opportunities we had left behind.

To make matters even worse and I think the biggest obstacle I had to confront was going to school with African-Americans. ***Please … pause here before you judge me!*** I know how horrible this sounds and I would not say it at all, but I need for you to truly grasp how this move affected me personally. Believe it or not, up until I got on that school bus for the first day of school, I had no recollection of being around people different than me. If I had, I certainly had no remembrance of it. Of course, being young, I could have simply not recognized it. At my age it was not something you gave much thought to. I saw a few African-Americans periodically when we would go somewhere in the car in Baltimore, but it was only a fleeting moment. My favorite teacher in Baltimore was African-American, but I did not see him that way. He was just my great music teacher who I grew very fond of and I missed dearly. His name was Mr. Stadium (I think?), and he was awesome!!! He took such interest in us and he had a way of making us laugh. We wanted to learn music because of him.

What is the deal here? Have my parents absolutely lost their mind? As you can see, I had a hard time adjusting to changes in my culture. I had problems on the school bus. Things simply were not working. As time would have it, after a short period of time things got better and I adjusted. I would not only adjust, but I would have an African-American as one of my dearest friends in high school. She was so beautiful and kind. She would spend many nights at my home during my school years. Much later in life, she would also attend my first wedding. I loved her like a sister … *imagine that!*

I got a lot of attention my first year in high school, or should I say in middle school. In Maryland I was leaving Holabird Junior High School and would have entered Dundalk Senior High School. In Virginia I was entering middle school as senior high did not start until the 10th grade. If I remember correctly, I was housed in the building with the 8th graders. Nevertheless, I was the new girl on the block and the boys loved flirting with me. People made fun of the way I talked. I had a different accent than they did, but I could not hear it. I remember getting one letter from a friend in Maryland. She made the comment she could tell I was changing because my letters were beginning to sound like a country person. *What does that mean? How could I 'sound' like a country person in a letter?* She said I used words differently or something … strange!

Being I felt so insecure and unsure of who I was or where I belonged, I enjoyed all the attention I was getting. I was meeting friends. Though I was still determined to go back to Berkshire as soon as I could, life got easier. I wish I could say it were all that simple. The move, my dad being gone so much, the lack of communication in my family, and so many, many other things caused me to harbor a lot of feelings inside of me which would make me vulnerable to situations I should never have been in to begin with.

Chapter Six

My dad would eventually join us permanently, and he would pour all his energies into the store him and mom founded. Overnight my parents would have more income than they dreamed possible. The store would prove to be such a success that we eventually bought a new home. New cars, new clothes, new everything was surfacing. But, as with all things that glitter and appear to be gold, this new success came with a lot of heartache and turmoil. My dad would spend almost every waking moment at the store. When he did come home, he would be drinking, and my safe-haven was now filled with even more arguing and strife. I could not wait for the sun to rise each morning. With it we would become the happy family all over again. Each of us focusing on what we needed to get through and going separate ways. We loved each other very, very much, but life would not be kind to us. We all seemed to make poor choices. There was no real guidance or helpful direction to follow, so we wandered. Every single member of my family was dealing with issues of their own, and we were all looking for what we needed wherever we could.

One thing never changed! I was still reminded daily of what my parents expected from me. A lot of their happiness was based on what I would become. It was as if they could somehow be happy and find fulfillment if I became all they dreamed for me.

My mom … well, I was her first daughter and she was determined I was going to make something of myself … be a lady and overcome everything in life she could not. I was going to have everything she never had. Both my parents tried to live out their lives through me, and at my age, this was a lot for me to handle. I kept telling myself I would do it or die trying. I did not realize it then, but I was already dying on the inside.

My dad did not have much of a relationship with his elder children from his first marriage, so he had a lot of hopes in the things I did. Periodically one or more of his children would come for an extended visit, but I do not have a lot of memories of spending a great deal of time with them until I got older. I would hear a lot of things, both bad and good, that influenced my life because of them. Dad's older children never seemed to want us around. The older I got, the more I realized just how much they resented us. As an adult, I would make an honest effort to bond with them because I truly cared about them. They were my siblings regardless of what happened between our parents, but they would never accept us. I finally had to realize that the closeness I longed to have with them would never be reciprocated. It is sad when I think about it. I wanted an older sister for myself just as I was an older sister to my younger siblings. I think we could have had some awesome times if everyone could have just let go of their pain and hurt and accepted each other for what we were. This would not be the case, and I think we all missed out on many fun family times because of it. Imagine how much a large family such as ours could have done together.

To this very day, I continue to pray for restoration for all my family. I hope I live long enough to see it. *(Note: Just recently ... and this is many years after writing the above ... I would learn that my half-brother passed away. Can you believe we were never notified of his passing? I was told that another half sibling took it upon themselves to keep this from us. They never even listed us as siblings in the obituary. At first, I was very angry and hurt. I wanted to lash out. Then my anger turned to love. I wanted to sit down and write a letter trying to penetrate the hard heart that had done this. After much prayer, God simply showed me that prayer was all I would be able to offer. I could not change them. I had been there for this individual through their bout with cancer. If that did not show my love, then no letter would do it now. Again, for whatever reason and though it makes no sense in light of how they treated us, I still love and care about them. I was so heartbroken to learn my brother had passed away. I would never get a chance to let him know how much I loved and cared about him. The urge to strike out at my half-sibling for what they chose to do was prevalent, but God ministered to my heart. If anything, I feel sorry for them. For most of their lives ... for the majority of my half-siblings' lives ... they have carried bitterness, anger, and hurt around over the demise of the marriage of our dad and their mom. They blamed us though we were not even around. They never found healing within themselves, so they directed all of their pain towards us. How sad! How very very sad!*

To make matters even worse, shortly after I was advised of the passing of my half-brother, I was told one of my half-siblings had lost a child. My heart broke! I have two other siblings who have been through this horrendous ordeal themselves. As a family unit, we could have been there to support them and bring much comfort and caring into their lives ... had we been allowed.)

Back to the boys and all the attention! It was great, and it was fulfilling a need inside of me that I had to be loved and to feel loved. Of course, I had more love at home than most children did, but it was not enough. The attention I was getting at school was wonderful and I looked forward to going to school. I could not wait for Mondays to come and I hated to see Fridays arrive. I was still too young to date and weekends were boring. I had to work in my dad's store when Mom was at home, and when my Mom was working at the store, then I had to be at home with the younger siblings. Either way, I had to shoulder responsibility that was simply too much for a child my age to carry. I feel the responsibilities I had to take on after we moved to Virginia, and being I was still a child myself, somehow robbed me of being a teenager. I could not be carefree like most children my age, and I have regretted this all of my life. It made me so much more aware of how I desired the carefree lifestyle for my children. I wanted them to be young for as long as they could.

I can remember once when a certain individual had made fun of the fact that my son still played with items they perceived as too immature for him. I simply responded that when my son was ready to lay these items down, then he would. I did not want him to grow up any faster than he had to. I do not regret the decision I made. He is a wonderful son, and I think he is right where he needs to be, as are both of my children.

During the first few months of being in the 9th grade, I would meet two different girlfriends I would bond with … both for different reasons. It would be ironic in some ways because these two girls were on different ends of society. One was from a very prominent family and looked like a porcelain doll. Her family lived on the hill beside the house we rented when we first came to Virginia. Their home was being built when we first moved in. As it took shape, steadily getting bigger and bigger, I thought I was going to live next door to the President or someone else who was very prestigious. Of course, this was only my imagination, but it was more of a house than I had ever lived in. The house had intercoms throughout all the rooms. It was three levels, had a two-car garage, and all the amenities you could possibly want in the early 70's. Up until this time, I originally thought my family was on the upper scale, but I would soon find out that this was not the case. Not in the beginning anyway.

The family who was building the house next door finally moved in and I would find a friend. Though she and I were as different as night and day, we bonded in other ways. We would spend the night at her house often. I cannot remember one time that she spent the night with me. It did not matter though because I had a friend. We laughed together. We cried over boys together. We even stole Kent cigarettes from her mom and smoked them in secret. I had a friend and life was looking up.

At this point, I want to share that about a year ago, after not communicating since graduation, this friend and I reconnected via Facebook. We are enjoying our new friendship and she has become very dear to me. She, too, is a Christian and we enjoy one another immensely. I cannot wait to be able to visit her some day or for her to visit me. We have discussed driving half way and meeting. We have talked about old times. She told me how much she always thought my bedroom was so beautiful. *Imagine that!* The girl who I thought had everything was admiring something I had. Just another example of how we can remember things so differently then they truly were.

As the school year progressed, I would meet my other friend. She was a totally different type of friend. She had a spirit that would not stop, and she was beautiful. My first friend was beautiful also, but in such a different way. This second friend reeked of sexual beauty. She could walk down the hallway and every eye, both boys and girls, would be on her. I can remember a time when my ex-husband and I were waiting on her to come out of her house as we were all going out together. As she walked to the truck, her hips swaying from left to right, my ex-husband looked at me and sort of shook his head. I smiled and said, *"She knows how to work it, doesn't she?"* She was just so special and different. Because of her beauty, she did not bond well with a lot of girls, so I was truly blessed to have her in my life.

At this particular period in my life, my second friend and I would bond even more than my other friend and I. One was the type of girl my parents wanted me to be, and the other was the type of friend I could expose my wilder side to. She loved to smoke cigarettes and she even drank. I have many memories of us hiding out in her aunt's cellar, smoking cigarettes and sipping on wine.

I had two friends which allowed me to be what I needed to be and what I wanted to be. How great was that? To make matters even more intense, they both would be after the same guy. I became their go-between, the one who tried to keep peace between them, and it made me feel important. I spent more time with my second friend. Friend #1 and I were fast friends, but our lives were on different social scales. Because of my obligations at home, I was not involved in extracurricular activities as she was. She was a cheerleader, a life guard at the community pool, and she did a lot of other things I was not included in. She also associated with individuals who did not care much for me. I was a newbie and not easily welcomed into their inner circle.

Those first few months of school proved to be better than I had ever dreamed, but the best was yet to come. I was soon to meet the boy that would turn my world around and become the most important person in my life for many, many years.

Chapter Seven

It started out as just another simple day. Friend #2 had invited me to go to a horse show with her behind the high school on the agricultural grounds. She wanted to meet up with this boy she was interested in and he had a friend. This meant she had to bring a friend. *Why not?* I did not have anything else to do. *Horses though! Yuk, but what the heck!* I thought it could prove to be fun. Little did I know that this day would take me down a totally different road and life would never be the same. I was just thankful my mom could be home, so I could go.

Saturday finally got here, and we arrived at the horse show. It was very different from anything I had ever attended. You never witnessed things like this in Baltimore. *Had I ever seen a real horse other than in a parade or on television*? Now these huge specimens were everywhere. I could not walk far without having to sidestep horse manure and the stench was overwhelming. *How could people function normally and be surrounded by such a smell as this? Is this what they thought was fun?* I hoped my friend knew I was only doing this for her. I told her she owed me big time!

We had been wandering around for a while checking things out. The horse show was hosted in a large oval shaped outside arena. The most interesting event to me was the barrel racing. It consisted of four barrels being placed at each end of the arena, along with two barrels across from one another in the middle of the arena towards the fence. There was enough space between the fencing of the arena and the barrels for a horse and rider to circle around them. The participants would enter the arena and go through the event in a circle eight shape. By what I could tell, they were judged by time, whether they cleared the barrels without making contact, and so forth. I admired those who were in this event as it scared me just watching them.

As we meandered around, my friend would introduce me to people she knew. Eventually, like zeroing in on a target, she spotted her prey. She turned on the charm, and off we went. If I could have communicated with boys like she did, well I would not have needed a friend. I never could figure out how she did it. She had to be the most personable person I had ever met. At times, I was literally mesmerized by her charm and easy-going nature. Of course, being as beautiful as she was did not hurt, that is for sure. She had the greenest eyes I had ever seen, and her eyelashes were so long and black. Though she wore make-up, she was as naturally beautiful as anyone I had ever known. I loved her. We laughed together, and I could tell her ANYTHIING!!! We painted each other's nails, did each other's hair, and we danced together. When we were together, we were unconquerable, and we were on top of the world. Finally, I had a friend to do things with as I had in Maryland.

This day, like many to come, would prove to sustain my position of being on top of the world. My friend had her eyes set on this boy and we moved forward. She approached him slowly, like a cat moving toward its prey. After moments of simply staring at one another, she came out of her reverie and introduced us. He, in turn, introduced both of us to his friend. When everyone moved a side and I could see his friend more clearly, I realized he was very cute. He looked wild as the horse he was trying to hold, with hair long and mangled, shirt unbuttoned down to the waist, and sweaty from competing in events. As cute as he was, I did not want to get near him. He stunk and smelled like hay. I did not want to look like that.

Nothing my friend did ever surprised me. She was so full of life and craved excitement. But when she advised me she wanted to go riding on those horses, I did not know how to respond. I thought to myself, "*You have got to be kidding!*" I was soon to find out just how serious she was. The next thing I knew she was atop the horse and they were gone. They were heading down the hill at a fast gallop. She was on the back holding on for dear life and loving it. All I could see was hair in the wind.

As I was watching them, I completely forgot about the other boy who was right behind me with his horse. He had never dismounted, and he continued to sit there. A few seconds later, I heard what I thought was a voice coming from over my shoulders. I turned towards him and realized he was speaking directly to me. I just was not sure I heard him correctly! *Excuse me … you want me to ride with you? Have you lost your mind? Ok, Janet, you either do this or you will be a real loser. You will look so foolish if you deny him the privilege. Do not let on how you are scared to death to pet this animal (the horse, of course, and not the boy), much less ride on the back of it.*

The other guy had a name and it was Donnie. Donnie was on the horse holding out his hand for me to get up. I thought to myself, "*Ok, here goes nothing*". If I lived to get off this animal, I would kill my friend wherever she was.

I was up, and we were off. I was holding onto Donnie so hard that I am not sure how he could be breathing. I had my head on his back, my arms around his waist, and I was praying for all I had. As Donnie sped faster and faster, I knew I would never EVER allow anyone to talk me into this again.

As you can guess, I survived not only the ride but the whole day. I came away head over heels in love and life would never be the same. Donnie was great, and I was sure he liked me too. I could not wait to get to school on Monday to see what would transpire.

I was so nervous the remainder of that weekend. I could not stop talking about Donnie. I thought Monday would never come. I did not think I would ever be so excited to go back to school, but I was. Never mind that I was supposedly still missing my boyfriend, Buddy, from Maryland. The thought of Buddy simply eluded me. I even wrote my friend in Maryland and told her all about my experience. I knew she would get a big kick out of it. I had to tell someone, and I knew I could not tell my parents.

Monday finally arrived. When I got up that morning, I made sure I looked the best I could. I was so excited about what the day would bring I did not even care that I had the responsibility for my younger siblings. Nothing could have spoiled the mood I was in. I made sure every hair was in place. I put on a little extra perfume, and I made sure my outfit was just perfect.

I am sure I had more patience with the care of my younger siblings on other mornings. On this day, I simply wanted to get them out the door and to the bus stop. I was on a natural high!!!

I arrived at school, and I acted like it was just another dreary day. I did not want to appear overanxious. As soon as I arrived at school, out of the corner of my eye, I was on the lookout for Donnie. The day would progress as usual, but I would never make contact with Donnie at any time. I later learned Donnie was housed in the other school building because he was older than me and in the 10th grade. Unlike my school in Maryland, the junior high school and the senior high school were adjacent to one another. Not so in Maryland. The schools were in two separate locations.

To make matters even worse, I found out Donnie was supposedly going steady with another girl. I kept telling myself this had to be a lie. *Where was his girlfriend on Saturday? Why was he flirting with me the way he did if he had a girlfriend?* My heart was broken, and then …

The day was almost over, and I was at my locker hunched over getting something from the bottom. I could sense someone was behind me. They were standing so close I could feel the heat radiating between us. As I was straightening up and turned to face whoever was behind me, I discovered Donnie. We were so close I thought he was going to kiss me. He was even cuter all cleaned up. My day was getting better.

We chatted for a bit, and then he asked me out. Obviously, what I heard about the girlfriend must have been wrong, and I said yes. He took my telephone number, and I was on cloud nine. To this day, I still have the slip of paper that Donnie wrote my telephone number on.

Now all I needed to do was talk my parents into allowing me to go out with a boy who was almost four years older than me. They had to say yes, or I would simply die. All the rest of the day I kept rehearsing in my mind what I would say to my parents when I got home.

Though my parents finally relented and said I could go if we double-dated, it took days of arguing before they agreed. Why they eventually changed their mind I will never know. I think realistically they just did not have the energy to keep arguing with me over this. They had their own issues to deal with, and I was not making life any easier. I also think it may have had something to do with trust. My parents had no reason to not trust me. I was only 13 at the time, but I sincerely think they thought I was mature enough to handle this. After all, I was taking on a lot of responsibility at home. I do not think they viewed me in terms of age. They saw the levels of responsibilities I had, and this deceived them into thinking I was more mature than I really was. I know in my heart if they had of known how this relationship would affect me, I am sure they never would have gone along with it. They were not being neglectful … just careless. They were giving me more credit than I could handle. Regardless of how responsible I was at home, I was still 13 emotionally and mentally.

Another reason I think my parents relented was because of everything that had happened up to this point. They knew I had been unhappy for so long, and I think guilt made them give in. They wanted to do something to put joy back into my life.

I thought it was great my parents agreed to let me go. I could not conceal my happiness. I was walking on air and daily anticipating our first date … *my first date*! Donnie could get his friend to ask my friend out, and we would be set for a double date. It would all work out.

Monday morning at school Donnie again met me at my locker. I excitedly told him I could go out. We set it up for the weekend, and I was giddy to the bone. To think I had to wait another few days to go out with this guy I was already in love with was more than I thought I could handle. We saw each other during the week at school. He would meet me at my locker in the mornings, and we would see each other throughout the day.

Can we pause here for a moment and reflect on something I have shared … ***I was in love****?* Can you imagine a girl of 13 years of age being in love? We do not even know what love is at that age. We have no idea of the responsibility or sense of commitment that comes with being in love. We are not in love but infatuated with what we perceive love to be. Worldly love is no comparison to the love God intends between a husband and a wife. God's love has nothing to do with the butterflies in your stomach or the romance you perceive love to be. It is about commitment … it is about forgiveness … it is about honoring Him and allowing Him to guide and lead you. It is about remaining focused when all the giddy feelings are gone … smiling when the children that have been produced from this 'love' have kept you up all night crying … supporting each other … listening to the hurts, pains, dreams, and desires of your partner … putting your own selfish desires on the back burner to lend a hand to your mate! I could go on and on, but I think you see where I am going with this. I was 13 and in love … it was like walking blindly towards the edge of a cliff with no knowledge I am about to fall off.

Friday finally arrived. I had bought a whole new outfit for the occasion. I remember my dress was baby blue and it buttoned down the length of the dress in the front. It had a belt around the waist, and I wore a scarf around my neck. It was the perfect outfit for the perfect date. It reminded me of the dress that Melonie Adams wore in *The Notebook*. It was the scene in which she returned to Noah when he had completed the house. She had spent the night with him. Even the stacks she wore looked like the ones I had picked out for my special date. When I saw this movie, this very day returned to my memory.

You will never for the life of you guess who helped me not only pick out the clothes I would wear, but also assist me in getting ready. They seemed to be genuinely excited for me and wanted to share in this chapter of my life. *Are you ready?* It was one of my half-siblings. They were visiting my dad on this weekend and I was glad to have them here. This is what was so confusing to me at times. Love would be shared here and there, and then nothing but anger and bitterness. I never knew what side of them I would get.

I was so excited about my date. I was thinking how much I would have liked for my friends in Maryland to see me now. I felt all grown up inside. Part of me was grown up beyond my years due to all the responsibilities I had in life, but now I truly felt ALL GROWN UP. Of course, you know, and I know, I was just 13 years of age and far from being grown up. I look at my son who is 16 today and I cannot even imagine him going on a date, much less having the responsibilities I had at his age. *(Note: My son is 19 today but when I wrote the above three years ago.)*

I remember when my daughter was young. We were very protective of her. I can remember after she did start to date how it worried me constantly. I did not want her to make the mistakes I made in life. I did not want her to have the responsibilities I had in life at her age. However, because of everything I had endured up to this point in life, I was not the mother to her I should have been. As my parents did with me, we gave our daughter all the material things we could but my presence in her life was missing.

Back to my big date ... Donnie picked me up on Friday evening and I know my feet were not touching the ground. I do not even remember if my parents were there to meet him. I truly do not think they were. It may have been because my older half-sibling and her husband were home with me. Donnie told me everyone was in the car, and I was very anxious to see my friend. I soon discovered that seeing my friend would have to wait for another time. As Donnie was holding the passenger car door open for me to get in, I glanced in the back to realize my friend was not there. In her place was another girl. As I sat down, Donnie's friend introduced his new friend to me. It was a bit awkward at first. I knew her from school, but we were not really friends. We would later become friends. Over the years I can remember being in her basement at her house many times listening to records. We had a lot of fun talking about our guys and just hanging out. Eventually, they married. I ran into her not long ago and it was great to see her. Donnie's friend ... her husband ... had passed away and I was truly sorry to hear this.

At this point, the fact that Donnie's friend brought someone else did not matter to me. Donnie was the only person I was really concerned about. I missed my friend and was disappointed we could not catch up, but my thoughts were elsewhere once I realized she was not coming along. Besides, she already had her eyes set on someone else, and I would be with Donnie.

It was April 29, 1971, when we met. On May 13, 1971, we started going "steady" ... shortly after our first date. It had been two weeks since the horse show. I was so lucky, and my world would forever be altered. Ironically, years later when I was contemplating a date for my future husband and I to get married on (not Donnie), I wanted to do it on April 29th. It was not possible, so I chose April 26th. *What in the world would possess me to think such a thing as I was getting ready to wed another person?* Just another example of how immature I truly was in life and how thoughtless I was about others. I do not think it was a lack of compassion towards others that I felt as much as it was that when it came to me and my happiness, I was pretty much self-centered. I loved my husband a great deal, but Donnie was always just a thought away.

After our first date, Donnie and I would become inseparable. Eventually he would meet my family, and I would meet his. We would go through many things, as all young couples do. Donnie was a bit on the wild side as a teenage boy. We would have problems with the ex-girlfriend, with him stepping out on me with other girls, with our arguing over silly and stupid things, but we would always work our way back to one another. He became my total source of happiness. I could talk to him about anything. He would also bond with a family member of mine, and they would become fast friends. I found in Donnie what I thought I was lacking in other areas of my life. He loved me, and he did many things to show me that love. I knew we would be together forever, and life could not be better.

I did whatever Donnie thought was best. If he thought my skirt was too short, I changed into something more appropriate. If he thought I had too much makeup on, I washed my face and adjusted my makeup to his liking. Please do not think Donnie was a controlling person because this was not the case. I chose to do all I could to make him happy. He became my best friend and my protector. He also became another person in my life that I had to please. In my mind, I had to be what he wanted me to be, just as I had to be what my parents thought I should be, or what others thought I should be. Thinking like this should have set a light off in my mind that this was not as life was intended to be. However, at my age, I did not care. I thought this was how it was supposed to be. It was not as if I could base our relationship on past experiences as I had none.

I was not allowed to date but one night on the weekend, and Donnie could only come to the house on Wednesday nights. I had responsibilities at home taking care of my younger siblings because my parents were busy with the store. I could not participate in sports or other events at school because I was needed at home. Though this was a far cry from my life in Baltimore, it was workable for me now because I had the best boyfriend any girl could want. It did not matter to me that my life was pretty much isolated from the rest of the world so long as I had Donnie. I did not need girlfriends or activities. Though the friends I had met, and I would remain in contact, we would not have many overnights any more. When I was allowed free time from my responsibilities at home, I wanted to spend it with Donnie. *I had to be the perfect daughter for my parents. I had to be the perfect older sister for my younger siblings. I had to be the perfect younger sibling for my older siblings. I had to be the perfect girlfriend for Donnie.* I did not feel overwhelmed though because Donnie loved me, and I loved him. Someday we would marry, and it would all work out.

Chapter Eight

Some things in the country were no different from the city. Having sex was rampant among my friends. It was an era of free love, love the one you are with, and the sexual revolution. It did not matter whether you lived in the city or the country, the world was the same on some levels regardless of where you lived. Sex, however, was one aspect of life I had not experimented with. After two years of dating, Donnie started putting pressure on me to sleep with him. He would break up with me, date other girls, go back and forth with his ex-girlfriend, and sex would become a big problem for us. I wanted to please Donnie, but I did not want to let my parents down. I felt like there was always a struggle going on in my mind. On one hand, there were my parents and everything I knew they wanted for me. Then, there was Donnie. I could not imagine my life without him. My reluctance to be intimate with him was causing him to doubt my love for him, or so this is what he constantly was drilling in my mind. Repeatedly, he would tell me I did not trust him or love him as much as he loved me. How gullible I was at that age! The four years difference in our age did not seem like much in the way of numbers, but it was a valley in the way of maturity. If my parents could not see this, then how was I to come to this conclusion? Yes, Donnie was four years older than me, but he was still immature himself.

Again, in defense of my parents, I truly think their inability to realize how detrimental this relationship was to me had something to do with trust … they trusted me to make rational decisions regardless of my age. I had appeared to be doing this up until now, so they had no reason to doubt I would not continue making good choices. Why would they think otherwise?

I say my parents were ignorant to what was going on, but in looking back, I get very confused about it all. I recall an evening I was home with the younger siblings. Both of my parents were working at the store. It was a Friday night, so Donnie chose to come to the house and babysit with me. I guess my parents felt comfortable with this set up because my younger siblings were there. At some point the siblings fell asleep. Donnie and I ended up on the sofa in the living room fooling around. My mom entered the house without us realizing it. We both jumped up, but it had to be obvious what was going on. Donnie was asked to leave, and we never spoke of it again.

In pausing here, I have to say how sad that it would be many, many years later in life before I would be introduced to Jesus Christ. How different my life would have been had I known Jesus Christ! My faith would have sustained me through these difficult decisions at such an early age. I see my nieces and nephews who have been raised in the Word. How different their dating years were compared to mine! For most, when they walked down the aisle to meet their future spouse, they had no sexual history trailing behind them. They have walked in His Word and they are now reaping the benefits of such a joyous union. Their marriages ... and the dating years for those still unmarried ... have been untainted by misguided desires.

I think my parents sensed Donnie and I were having issues, but we never ever talked about them. Regardless, they had to know something was amiss because I was spending more and more Saturday nights at home. I am sure they could hear me crying in my room quite a bit. My mom's patience with me had worn thin because I was not holding up my duties at home as I should have been. She would constantly tell me how silly I was acting, and how all of this was just part of growing up. *How could she say that to me? Did she not realize how much Donnie meant to me? Did she not realize how badly I was hurting him by not sleeping with him? Did she not realize that Donnie did not want to date other girls, but I was not giving him much choice? Did she not realize all the love that I felt was lacking in our home I was now getting from Donnie?* No! My mom did not understand these things. She had issues of her own she was dealing with. She did not have time to deal with this adolescent stuff. I needed to grow up and get over it. I knew this, but I simply could not do it. Just the thought of not having Donnie in my life sucked the breath out of me. When I thought about it, I would literally get sick to my stomach. I had to make this right.

To give you an example of how much I obsessed over Donnie and his influence in my life, I remember a time when we were in the front of my house. Donnie and I had gotten into a disagreement over something and he turned away from me as if to leave. Panic set in. I literally got down on the sidewalk and held him by his legs, so he would not leave me. *How sick is that*? It had to be an obsession because normal girls do not react as this. I had to be very insecure in life. I could never for the life of me imagine my daughter or any young girl acting in this manner. This should have been a warning sign to someone that I, every bit the age of 15 now, was way over my head and needed help! As a parent, I know how I would have reacted were this my child. *Did my parents witness this?* I would have to say no. Knowing my dad as I did, he would have flipped out. My mom would never have tolerated this type of behavior. As much as she was weak at times and fought depression, she could also be tough as nails. She expected the same from me. This would have been totally unacceptable to her.

As I stated earlier, Donnie and I would go back and forth, but he must have loved me because he always returned to me. On this day he would come back and make me the happiest girl in the world. He showed up at the house to pick me up for what I thought would be another date of arguing about sex. As much as I dreaded going, I was ecstatic he was giving me another chance. He did love me, and my parents had to see this. Why would he keep coming back if he did not love me?

As I am typing all of this, I find myself getting embarrassed at just the thought of sharing such personal information with strangers. I am so not this person today. Knowing my daughter, my son, my nieces, my nephews, and so forth may read this book makes me wonder how they will feel about me. It has always been a battle within me from the moment God placed it upon my heart to write it. In the Bible, God explains to us the purpose of hardships and storms in life. He encourages us in Mark 5:19 to go home to our friends and share with them how much He has done for us. My favorite is Psalm 30:11-12, *"You have turned for me my mourning into dancing; You have put off my sackcloth and clothed me with gladness, To the end that my glory may sing praise to You and not be silent. O Lord my God, I will give thanks to You forever."* If my afflictions in life will minister to one person what God can do in their life and give them hope where there is none, then my embarrassment is well worth it.

On this particular night, Donnie picked me up and we went to the movies. Afterwards we went to the local hamburger place to eat. We had these two special seats we always sat in when we ate there. As an adult, I have returned to the same place many times. As I remember the years past, I chuckle to myself. I even wonder from time to time if our names are still etched in the bottom of the counter as they once were.

After we finished eating, as always, we went parking. I had butterflies in my stomach, but Donnie was different on this night. He did not try anything, but only told me how much he loved me. He shared with me again how he wanted to spend the rest of his life with me. We talked about our dreams of someday being married and how it would be. He was contemplating quitting school and getting a job. This way he could work and save up some money. Eventually we could get married and start a life of our own. Of course, I had to graduate first. We had big plans for our future.

What happened next would only confirm our true intent to be together forever … Donnie did not pressure me about sex, but instead he gave me a beautiful pre-engagement ring. I became the happiest girl in the world. The ring was beautiful. It was silver with a tiny diamond in the middle. It was not much but to me it was the same as a huge diamond. He had already given me a black onyx ring for my birthday and now this. My parents would now have to realize just how much Donnie loved me and this was not just some childish game we were playing. He placed the ring on my finger and I could not wait to get home to show it off.

When we arrived back at my house, I showed the ring to my mom. She simply said it was pretty. The next day I would show it off to my dad before he left for the store. It was then my parents would tell me not to let this ring go to my head and it was nothing more than a piece of jewelry. I could not understand what they meant by that? Could they not see that Donnie and I were serious about marriage? We were going to get married as soon as I graduated. Of course, I could never say this to my parents because college was the only option for me as far as they were concerned. This is what they had planned, and they could not see it any other way. If they even thought I was contemplating another direction for my life, one in total opposition to their dreams, then it would be over for Donnie and me right then and there. As was the norm, I kept this to myself and never confided in my parents about it or anything else.

Donnie and I would continue to see one another as much as we could. He would quit school and go to work for a construction company that another member of my family worked for also. We still had problems and broke up every now and then, but we always got back together. Sex would no longer be an issue because I finally relented. I had to, or I would lose him. Besides, we were going to be husband and wife anyway, so why not? It did not solve all our problems like I thought it would, but it was my guarantee that Donnie would never leave me.

How sad that a young girl is so desperate for love that she would lose all sense of dignity and sense of morality to hold on to someone? Without my life being God-centered, there was no hope for me to find a sense of security in anything else. I would make many mistakes throughout my life that came with a high price. I am just thankful to Christ that I now strive to raise my son by lessons learned through my mistakes as a young adult. With Christ at the center of my life and guiding me as to how to parent my son, we are making headway in areas I never thought about as a child. I did not have as solid a foundation when I raised my daughter, but I was much more open with her about dating than my mom was with me. My mom did not have a lot of guidance in her life when she was growing up. I now understand her in more ways than I ever did. Though she was an adult and married, she was not knowledgeable in a lot of things. She did not have a simple childhood, and because of this, I ask you again to not judge my parents too harshly. Parents cannot teach their children things in life if they are ignorant of these things themselves. My parents gave the best they had at this stage of their lives, and I am blessed to have had them. What they lacked in parental guidance they overachieved in love. Because of that, my siblings and I love each other dearly and we are there for one another. I would rather have that than anything else.

When both my parents had passed, four of us siblings had scheduled a time to meet and go through their house and dispose of their belongings. During this transaction, we never had so much as a cross word. Everything was settled peaceably. As a person who has worked for attorneys the majority of my adult life, I can tell you that being able to do this without arguing was a huge credit to the love my parents instilled in us. Many families, with only two or three children, cannot settle their parents' estate without bickering or ending up in court. I have seen this more times than I care to remember, and I always thought how truly sad it was.

If my parents knew Donnie and I had been intimate, they never said anything. I am sure my older brother did not know because he would have been very upset over it, or I think he would have been. Donnie and one of my brothers were still best friends, but I am sure Donnie never shared things with him about our personal relationship.

Chapter Nine

At the age of 15 life seemed to be as good as it could get. Donnie and I had been dating for a little over two years. Everyone knew we were a couple, and I was happy. As responsible as I had to be at home, when I was with Donnie, I was carefree and did not worry about anything. He took care of me. He loved me. He bought me pretty things. He treated me like a lady. He made it clear that I was priority in his life. Life was what I thought it should be. *What could possibly go wrong?*

Sex was never talked about in our home, so discussions of safe sex and contraceptives were totally out of the question. How could my mom talk about something I do not think she ever learned to be comfortable with? How could she discuss sex considering what she had endured herself at the hands of distant male relatives? This was alright though. Donnie was older than me and he knew what he was doing. I relied upon him to make sure nothing went wrong, and because he loved me, I knew everything would work out. Lack of maturity enabled me to not dwell on possible consequences of our actions. I simply was enjoying life and was ignorant enough to think it would always be this way.

Donnie and I never used contraceptives or none that I could remember. I simply relied on my trust in Donnie. I never worried about any of this because I trusted Donnie more than anyone in the world. He had taken care of me up to this point, and I knew he would never allow anything to happen that would hurt me. He knew what it would do to me, and how my parents would never forgive me.

I can imagine at this point in the book you are saying to yourself, *"Is this girl for real? Does she truly believe all of this"?* My answer to you is a simple, *"yes"*. I believed it all. It was as real for me then as life is for me now. I was that naïve, but more than that, I was that insecure. Though I knew my parents loved me more than life itself, their lack of a physical presence in my life left a void I continually tried to fill for many years. All the material things were great, but today, as a parent and mother, I can tell you emphatically that the presence of my parents in my life would have counted for so much more. Again, and I cannot say this enough, I understand everything my parents did. They struggled to give us what they lacked in life and what they thought was important. If they had grown up with the material things and not in poverty as they had, then I think things would have been different. We always try to give our children what we feel we lacked. They lacked the material things in life, so they strived to provide those things for us.

It never occurred to Donnie and me what we would do if something happened. We never discussed such things. I can tell you without a moment's hesitation that my parents would never ever have allowed us to continue seeing one another if they had known for certain we were intimate, much less if I turned up pregnant. I realize this may be in opposition to what I shared earlier about my mom walking in on Donnie and I, but I truly from the bottom of my heart think my mom knew we were only fooling around. I think she continued to trust that I would make the right decisions. I can only conclude that this train of thought was much easier for my mom than the alternative of discussing sex with me. It was a taboo subject in our home, and one that my mom was very uncomfortable with.

The very thought of ever becoming pregnant horrified me. I just pushed it to the back of my mind where we put things we do not want to deal with.

Sometimes in life we can push things to the back of our minds and think they will go away if we do not discuss them or think about them. We live our lives in denial. We never deal with the "what ifs" of life, and we never allow ourselves to really weigh the consequences of our actions. We just do what is pleasing for us at the time and never think beyond that moment. We live in a world that teaches us to go with the flow, enjoy the moment, and worry about the consequences only if and when you are faced with them. We walk on thin ice, allowing the roll of the dice to dictate our futures. My ice was soon to break, and the consequences would far outweigh any of the joys that led up to it.

Today, as I raise my son, I strive to have an open relationship with him. I am constantly reminding him that things he does and says are his choice. Every day, in everything he does, it is his choice. Making bad choices reaps bad consequences and it effects more than just him. I am a stickler on these things. I want him to always realize this and be considerate of how his choices in life are not all about him.

Looking back and being totally honest with myself, one would think that what I had heard about one of Donnie's ex-girlfriends would have been enough to make me realize how immature I was. I was told she had gotten pregnant and had an abortion. I am not sure to this very day if it were true or not, but just hearing it should have had some effect on me. I guess I simply did not want to believe it. If I chose to acknowledge this may have occurred, then I would also have to believe Donnie was part of it and he allowed this situation to happen.

What would that say about all the trust I had in him? It was much simpler for me to just ignore all of it and believe it was not true. *(Note: As an adult and many years later, I would have the opportunity to speak with Donnie about this ex-girlfriend. If she was pregnant, he said he had no knowledge of it. I have no reason to believe otherwise.)*

Donnie was no longer attending school. Each morning as I exited the school bus at the high school, I would go straight for the pay telephone that was located directly out front of the main doors. Donnie would call me each morning before the school bell rang. It was the first thing I thought of each day. This day would be very different from all the other days. I had to discuss something with Donnie and just the thought of doing so made me ill.

Up until that morning, I had been wrestling with this unsettling feeling in the pit of my stomach. I was a few days late for my monthly cycle, but I kept pushing it aside. I knew it would come so I never mentioned it to anyone, not even Donnie. *Why upset him over no big deal?* Sooner rather than later, those few days turned into a month and now I was scared in a way I had never been. I got off the bus that morning knowing I had to tell Donnie what I suspected. *What would he say? Why am I worrying about this?* Donnie had always taken care of me and he would not fail me now. Everything would work out. How it would work out I did not know. I just simply knew they would.

As was the custom each morning when I arrived at school, I got off the bus and went straight to the telephone. Shortly thereafter it rang. I thought my heart had stopped and my hands were shaking as I reached for the telephone receiver. My emotions were instantly calmed just hearing

Donnie's voice. It completely settled the upheaval in the pit of my stomach. Hearing him say, "*Good morning, baby*" made my world bright and sunny again. My doom would soon return as I wondered in my mind if everything were right with the world, then why was I having such a difficult time communicating with Donnie and getting the words out of my mouth. Normally I could tell Donnie anything, but sharing this with him was scaring me. Was it really telling him that was scaring me or was I deluding myself? I simply could not think beyond this moment. Could it be I was not just afraid of telling him, but I was fearful of it all?

Finally, I just convinced myself it would be fine. I needed to just open my mouth and the right words would come out. I prayed for courage and decided I had to tell him now. I do not remember how long it took me to convey to him what was happening. I just remember that after I did, the line went completely silent. *Ok, Donnie, any time now you can start reassuring me everything will be alright. Any time now you can start telling me you will take care of everything and we will get through this.* Still nothing. Complete silence! I was not even sure if Donnie was still on the line.

What seemed like forever only dragged out more and the silence was deafening. Finally, I said, "*Donnie, are you there?*" He simply said yes and that he had to go, or he was going to be late for work. The line went dead and there I stood holding the receiver in my hand. This was not the way this conversation was supposed to go. *Now what? How was I ever going to get through this day?*

All day in the back of my mind I convinced myself everyone knew. Somehow, I was wearing this *I am pregnant look* and the whole school could see it. I felt so ashamed and paranoid. *How did this all happen to me? Didn't Donnie know this was not supposed to happen? Was my trust misplaced in him?*

I am not sure exactly how the days or moments proceeded from that time on, but at some point, Donnie and I decided to try a pill that was on the market which supposedly would help girls' monthly cycles to start if they were late. They were called "Humphreys 11" and Donnie purchased some for me. I began taking them immediately, and now our morning telephone calls would start with, *"Anything yet*?" Days would pass, and nothing happened. To say our relationship was strained would be putting it mildly. I could not remember when we smiled or laughed during this time. We went from this free-loving happy couple to two people at a loss of words to share with one another. Donnie still reassured me he loved me, that he would not desert me, but whether I believed this was a different story. If I did not believe it, I never admitted it to myself. Donnie and I had something special and not even this would tear us apart. We would get it all back. We just had to get over this hurdle.

Assuming the worse, we discussed all our options … abortion, having the baby, adoption, marriage. We talked about it all, but the conversations always ended up with us fighting. *How could I make such a decision?* I knew nothing about abortions. I could not imagine me raising a child at my age. As for marriage, I just did not know. Give the child up … how could I even do that? *What about my schooling? What about me going to college? Where was all this leading?* I had no answers. Even though I always said I would never go to college because Donnie and I would marry, now that this was happening I was wondering about my parents' plans for me.

Donnie thought it was time we go to my parents. I simply did not see that as an option. They must never ever know. I was not rationally thinking because if I had been I would have realized just how unrealistic my thoughts were at this time. *Did I really think I could keep this from my parents?* Nevertheless, telling my parents was definitely not the way to go. No amount of talking would change my mind. *Did Donnie not realize what this would mean for me?* Up to this point, I was daddy's little girl. I was pure in my daddy's eyes and I could never disappoint him. My mom was depressed enough about life. What would this do to her? I could not allow this to happen. My parents lived their lives building my future. I was going to college. I was going to be someone in life. I was going to be that daughter dad walked down the aisle in the white wedding dress. *How could I destroy their dreams for me? How would I ever look at them again?* They would hate me. They would disown me. I could not and would not tell them. I could not disgrace them in this way. They deserved more. They had enough on their plates as it was, and I was their one hope in a world that was not turning out as they had planned. ***Please do not make me do this. I would rather die***.

Donnie and I finally decided we had to talk to someone, so we choose to share this with certain members of his family. We thought they would know what to do and they did. First off, they scheduled me an appointment with a doctor and they took me. It was confirmed. I was almost two months pregnant. We had to decide what to do and we had to decide **NOW!** A plan was set into motion and we had to move fast.

Of course, 'fast' was not fast enough. Time just seemed to fly by and we had no concept that while we lingered with this plan and that plan, the life inside of me was steadily growing. Before we knew it, I was approaching being three months pregnant. I could not button my pants anymore. Little did I know, but deep down inside of me, I was happy about this baby. I did not want to be. I could never ever say I was, but I could not help it. It was as if my stomach had a mind of its own. Now I was forever wrestling with what I knew I had to do and what I fantasized about. Of course, I was too young to realize that 'yes, the fetus inside of me did have a mind of its own' and it did have a life. I lacked the maturity to even contemplate these things. I did not know what the Bible said about anything, much less about this. We had to do something, and the clock was ticking faster with each passing day.

By now school had let out for the summer. To the best of my knowledge, we had a plan and were moving forward. I would tell my parents I was going away for the weekend with certain individuals who my parents would trust, and we would go have an abortion. Seemed simple enough. We would go away and come back with everything taken care of. No one would ever know, and life would return to normal. I could return to school in August and be that happy girl I once was. Never mind all my responsibilities at home. I would gladly continue with them in place of what I was now dealing with.

Years later as a mature adult, mother, and grandmother, I would get an opportunity to become involved with the local chapter of The Pregnancy Center. It was always a desire for me for obvious reasons. I found out during this time just how many young girls, young mothers, and mature women would have abortions simply on the premise that they could and then all would be done. They sadly learned that it was not that simple, and it was far from being over simply because of a medical procedure. Living with it all afterwards was the real battle.

Something just was not settling right in the pit of my heart. I remember being at my girlfriend's house shortly before our planned get-away, and we were laughing at the bump in my stomach. I had on these white pants I always wore, and I could not button them. My girlfriend and I were fantasizing about the baby, about names, whether it was a boy or a girl, and I remember laughing as I had not laughed in such a long time. *What in the world was I doing?* I do not know. I truly did not know. A plan was in motion and we had to go with it. I could not disappoint my parents like this. I could not continue to be pregnant, and I had to do what was right. Abortion was right, **right**? Someone please tell me!

I truly think the biggest obstacle in all of this was our hesitation to speak with a mature adult about the situation. If we could have had someone to turn to and discuss this situation with (i.e., a pastor, a guidance counselor, our parents), then I think we would have made better choices. As it was, you had a 15-year-old girl and a very immature young man trying to deal with a drastic life issue that neither of them knew anything about. Sure, I dreamed of this perfect couple living in this cute little house with an adorable baby and living happily ever after. However, let's get real here … that is exactly what it was … a DREAM!!! This was a real life we were messing with, but what did we know?

I, of course, was bouncing back and forth mentally from dream world to reality. In one of my confused states of thinking we could live happily ever after, I actually picked out the name for our child. If it was a boy, it would be James Michael. If it were a girl, it would be Sarah Renee.

Now, not only was I pregnant, but I had made the big mistake of allowing this pregnancy to take on a life. What did I know about any of this at the age of 15? I have learned as a parent that children at this age know it all. There is nothing you can teach them.

I was constantly wrestling with the decision we had made and the visions of this child in my head. It had a name now and yet I was going to destroy it. How conflicting this was for me! It was bad enough to be pregnant, but now I was pregnant and torn. I did not understand what was happening to me. I did not understand what I had done to myself by giving this pregnancy a name. I had no inkling the significance of this situation.

After the decision had been made for me to get an abortion, we got permission from my parents for me to go away for the weekend. Donnie and I ceased talking about it at all. Looking back, I have to wonder who actually made the decision to have the abortion. I cannot for the life of me remember. *Did I make the decision on my own? Did Donnie?* I find it hard to believe Donnie did, but yet how could I? I was in too much turmoil to make such a decision. Donnie eventually made a life altering decision he never could have made if the decision to abort this child had been his. I am back to square one … *who made the decision*? I guess it did not really matter.

Once the decision to have an abortion had been settled, whenever Donnie and I were together you could cut the tension between us with a knife. He tried to reassure me everything was going to work out. He was constantly telling me he loved me, but even though I heard his words, I did not believe them. Something was wrong with him. I could not figure it out. I would find out what it was sooner than I wanted to. Up until this point, Donnie and I never had problems discussing anything. We could talk about stuff most people did not share. Donnie had his own issues to contend with in life. I was all screwed up in my home life. We always sought solutions together. We talked about how we would do things differently if we ever got married. Now, all at once, there was this huge void between us. It did not feel good to me. I did not know how to handle it. His constant reassurance that things were fine and would work out was not putting my mind at ease.

Chapter Ten

Not long after we had made the decision to have an abortion but prior to actually leaving for the weekend, I was at my girlfriends' spending the day when my mom called me home. I could tell she was upset, and it scared me. *What in the world has happened now?* My family was forever having to deal with issues. Again, to say we were dysfunctional is over simplifying it, and now I had to deal with a family crisis on top of everything else.

My girlfriend's father drove me home. As we entered the driveway, my stomach hit an all-time low. There in the driveway was Donnie's car. *What in the world was he doing here?* Then, to scare me even more, my dad's car was home. Why wasn't he at the store? I thought to myself, *Oh my gosh, something horrible has happened*. I got out of the vehicle. Even as I walked up the sidewalk to the house, I knew what was going on, but I did not want to admit it. I just knew what I knew, and my entering the house confirmed it to me.

Before I got pregnant, Donnie and I talked about the children we would have after we got married. We talked about this a lot. I knew he had this love for children that was so beautiful. Whenever he was around children, he loved playing with them and seemed to never get tired. I knew someday he would make a wonderful father. Many years later, years after this had played out in our lives and we were separated and married to other people, Donnie's name came up in a conversation about him having children. My mom made the comment that she bet Donnie was a great dad. Even she felt he would be a great dad just from knowing him.

However, the idea of Donnie being a good dad was not on my mind when I got pregnant. We never talked about this pregnancy as a child. It was a problem that needed to be dealt with. Again, I was only 15. I was a child myself. I was so ignorant about fetuses, about having a baby, about giving birth or about anything relating to this subject matter. Never once while the plan was being made did Donnie ever say a word, hardly about anything. He just agreed with things and went along. I just thought he was at a loss for words, as we often were during this time. Never in a million years did I realize that Donnie's conscience was getting the best of him and he was contemplating telling my parents. I was soon to learn it was and he had.

I stood on the porch feeling physically ill, but I knew I had to go in. I worked up the courage to reach for the front door handle and I opened the door to complete silence. When I entered the living room, I could no longer deny what I already knew. The air was like this thick heaviness which wanted to suck the breath out of me. I kept telling myself to just breathe. As I turned my head to the right to look towards the kitchen, there was my dad sitting at the table. He was in the chair he always sat in, but he was just sitting there slouched over with his head in his hands. I could not tell if he was crying or not, but I sensed if he wasn't, then he had been. He did not even look up when I entered the house. *Do you know what that did to me?* Everything in me wanted to run to him and comfort him. My daddy was everything to me … he was my hero … I was his little girl. Just remembering this now as I type it for this book is making me sick to my stomach. I loved my daddy and the last thing I ever wanted to do was bring him shame or hurt him in any way. *What in the world have I done? My heart was breaking into a thousand little pieces!*

I was brought back to reality when I heard my mom's footsteps approaching the living room. I then turned to look in her direction, and you could tell she had been crying. Her eyes were all red and swollen. I assumed she had been in her bedroom, lying on the bed when I entered the house. Now as she got closer to me, she just stopped and stood there, looking at me as if she did not know who I was. *What did I expect?* I did not know who I was any longer. I did know, however, that I was the reason for her red eyes and the pain written all over her face. *How could I ever forgive myself for this?* I had broken the two most important people in my life.

All of this transpired in what I am sure was less than five minutes though it seemed like it was forever. Time seemed to stand still. My focus on my mom and dad made it possible for me to neglect the realization there was a third person in our midst. I did not see him at the time, but Donnie was sitting in the living room on the sofa.

I realized I had not even shut the front door, and as I did, Donnie stood up. He came towards me with his arms outstretched to hug me, but my mother stepped in front of me and said to him, *"I think you need to leave".* He slid in between the two of us and kissed me. He simply said I am sorry as he turned to leave. He reached for the doorknob and then he turned around. In that split second, I could see all this pain in his eyes. He too had been crying. He reached for my hands and said, *"Janet, I love you and I hope you know that. I am not leaving you and I never will. I just could not go through with this. I am sorry."* (Note: I wish I could tell you that my memory is this good; however, it is not. I have kept journals for most of my life. When we lost our home to fire, my journals were not destroyed. I have them to this very day. God had a purpose all along.)

Donnie turned to leave, and the door shut. I did not know if the explosion in my head was from the door shutting or if it was the sound of my heart breaking. I could feel this horrible fear in the pit of my gut, and it was travelling at a fast pace up my throat. It finally reached my mouth and I became violently sick. I stood in front of the door in the living room, bowed my head, and began vomiting. I thought I was dying.

My mom was a bit startled, but as any loving mother would, she rushed to take care of me. When she had realized I was throwing up, she went and got a cold rag for me to wipe my face. She cleaned up the mess and I just stood there. I do not think I could have moved if I wanted. What happened next, I am not sure. I have tried to replay it in my head, but I cannot seem to see it clearly anymore. I remember my mom hugging me as she started to cry again. I wanted to tell her how sorry I was, but the words would not come. My dad simply got up, put his hat on, turned towards the kitchen door, and left. I can only assume he had returned to the store. How many hours passed as I stood in my mom's arms? I do not know. *How many days passed before I saw Donnie again?* I do not know. I do know I spent a lot of days in my room crying. All around me there was nothing but silence in the house. My siblings seemed to have disappeared. Worst of all, my dad did not have much to say to me when he would come home.

My parents' bedroom was sort of adjacent to mine from an angle. From the walls of my room, I heard a lot of talking in hushed tones coming from their room. Several times, I heard my mom on the telephone. I never asked questions because I did not want answers. I was never sure what was going on. I do remember my parents seemed to cease with the arguing.

Unlike our normal day to day life, now they were a team working together.

What seemed like forever but in reality was only a few days, my mom came to me and said Donnie and I were getting married. She had been in conversations with Donnie's mom. We were to meet Donnie and his mom at the courthouse to get a marriage license. *Was I supposed to be excited?* I do not know. I had not spoken to Donnie since he left the house days ago. I was feeling like a puppet at this point, doing what I was told and never saying a word. I remember all the conversations Donnie and I had about marriage, and the joy I got just talking about it. *Where was that joy now? Why did this not feel right? Why did I suspect my mom was not being totally honest with me?* She was too nonchalant about the entire situation. Even as we drove to the courthouse, I knew this was not over. There were missing pieces to this puzzle, and I could not quite figure it out. I was too tired to even try.

On the way to the courthouse, we never spoke. My dad drove, my mother rode in the front with him, and I was in the back. I do not think any of us said a word. I do not even remember my parents speaking to one another. They just stared into space. I just felt numb. I played in my head, as I had many times in the past, the wedding I thought I would have someday. I could envision my dad walking me down the aisle to meet the man I knew I could not live without … Donnie. I could see the white gown I would be wearing. I could feel the excitement my mom and I would share as she helped me get dressed for my big day. Now, instead of walking me down the aisle, my dad was driving me to a courthouse to get a license to be married somewhere … someday … some way! *How would this even play out?* I had no clue and I most definitely was not going to ask questions. I was in the twilight zone and I did not know how to return to my life … the life before all of this. I wondered to myself if my life would ever be the same. How could it be … I was never going to be the same!

Looking back at my dismay over relocating to Virginia, I now thought if we could magically make this pregnancy go away I would never complain about the move again. Considering what I was going through now, our move was nothing in comparison.

We finally pulled up at the courthouse. What should have been a 15-minute drive seemed like hours. As we slowed to turn into the parking lot, I spotted Donnie's mother's car. In the front on the passenger side of the car was Donnie. He looked so much older to me and so very sad. I could not see his dad and I wondered where he was. I found out, as we exited the cars, that Donnie's dad had not come. I can only imagine what he must have said to Donnie about this situation. Donnie's dad was a Pentecostal preacher. He was from the old school and preached mostly on hell and damnation. Donnie and his dad, as most young boys at Donnie's age, had a difficult relationship periodically, so I am sure this did not help the situation between them. Just another thing for me to feel guilty about! I would carry a lot of guilt around for a very long time for what I had done to so many people. In a split second of time, I had caused more pain to others than most people cause in a lifetime, or so I thought. Never mind that I could not have caused this alone. I had a knack for assuming guilt on my own for things that happened, even if I was not the only one involved.

Donnie never exited the car to greet me. Only my parents, Donnie's mom, and I went into the courthouse. Donnie entered a short time thereafter. He came to where I was sitting and sat down beside me. He reached over and took my hand. From his hand, I felt all the love and reassurance I needed. I could physically feel my body become all warm inside. I was momentarily full of peace, but it would be short lived. Donnie loved me, and he was not going to leave me. We were going to be together and we were going to get through this. I had to hold on to this feeling even if it did not last for long.

As Donnie and I sat on the bench in the Clerk's Office, my parents and his mom went to the counter to request a marriage license for us. I heard them whispering, but I could not for the life of me hear what was going on. They were handed some papers and given instructions I did not hear. As they turned towards us, they motioned for Donnie. Donnie let go of my hand and got up. His mom, my parents, and he went into a courtroom and shut the door. I was left alone in the lobby wondering what in the world was going on. As I looked around at my surroundings, I felt as if every eye in the building was upon me. I could see and sense all the condemnation and accusations everyone was thinking. You got to know this was only in my mind, but it was very real for me at the time. I wanted the floor to open and consume me.

It seemed like forever they were in that courtroom. I should have just gotten up and went to see what was going on, but I did not. I could not move. My body again became chilled. I felt as if I weighed more than I could possibly lift off the bench, so I remained seated. Finally, they exited the courtroom, but no one looked happy or said anything directly to me.

My parents walked towards me and motioned for me to get up. Like the robot I had become, I followed them out of the courthouse and back to our car. I did not see where Donnie and his mother had gone. *Did they exit out of a different door?* As I walked to the car, I could still see Donnie's mother's car in the parking lot, but they were not in it.

Years later I would learn from Donnie what really transpired in that room. He advised me they went before a judge. The judge was asking Donnie questions about his intentions towards me. He asked Donnie if he was the expectant father, to which Donnie replied that he was. He also asked what Donnie's plans were at this time. Donnie responded that he was living at home with his parents and working. His intent was for us to get married and live with his parents until we could save enough money to move. Of course, this never took place. To this day neither Donnie nor I know why. Who made the decision on that day that contradicted everything which took place before the judge, but most importantly, who made the decisions that altered the course of my life forever?

All I could remember from that day was my sense of security being shattered once again. Even thought our parents were there to sign showing we had their permission, because I was under 16 we could not get married unless I stated I was pregnant. At that time, young girls under 16 could only get married if they were pregnant. Pause for a moment and take into consideration that this is being shared with me **after** we have left the courtroom. No one bothered to ask me while we were still there, *"Are you pregnant?"* I do not know how I would have responded, but it was obvious to me I would never have an opportunity to respond for myself. Other people were making my decisions before I was even brought into the equation.

Why was this happening to me? Why can they not just give us the license and let us go? Why are they making this so difficult? I could see by the look in my mom's eyes and the despair on my dad's face that I could not go along with this. I knew in my gut they wanted me to say no ... that I could not go public with this pregnancy. How could I hurt them anymore than I already had? I could not put my family through this public humiliation. I could not, and I would not. They had suffered enough in life as it was, and I would not make things any harder on them! I loved Donnie with every fiber of my being, but even that was not enough to make me hurt my parents any more than I had already.

I keep saying how I would not put my parents through this ... how I felt they had endured so much up to this point, but neither you nor I can take for granted this is how they felt. I was a 15-year-old girl **assuming** I had all the answers ... assuming I knew how everyone felt. Yes, I do believe all the adults involved could have taken on a more positive role in this situation, but we were all assuming things and no one really knew for certain. Today I see no fault here. I see a lot of immaturity on the part of Donnie and me, and I see a lot of pain and disillusionment on the part of our parents. There simply was too much confusion for anyone to think rationally.

What is very confusing about all of this is the fact that when the baby was due in January, I would have been 16. Why did we not simply wait to get married afterwards? I guess getting married was not the issue. The issue was my pregnancy and hiding it. We could not go public with such a travesty. What would people think of me ... what would they think of my parents? These were the real issues though no one was saying them.

Where was Donnie? I needed to talk to him, but he was not around. *Were they keeping us apart on purpose? How could I make this decision on my own? Was I even given an opportunity to make any decisions?* These questions would be answered by the devastation I saw all around me, and worse yet, the devastation that I felt in the pit of my soul. *How could I admit to the world I was pregnant? How could I disgrace my family and Donnie's family in such a way?* Donnie's father and mother were church-goers. They would hate me forever. I needed to talk to Donnie. *Where was he?* I simply opened the door to our car, sat down, and I cried. My parents remained standing outside of the car. Shortly thereafter, they joined me in the car and we left. I guess Donnie went home with his mom because I never saw him again that day, or for days to come.

Chapter Eleven

I wish I could remember more about the in-between times, but I simply cannot. I guess they are not relevant to what took place, but I cannot even remember what I was doing with myself now that school was out for summer break. I just remember returning to the house and feeling like the most horrible human being on the face of the earth. It is all so fuzzy to me now.

Did my parents and I talk? No! *Did my mom and I have some heart-to-hearts about all of this?* No! I returned to the four walls of my room and cried more than I thought humanly possible.

From here on out, I simply went through the motions of life. I did what I was told. I knew Donnie had returned to work, because my brother told me. *Why was Donnie not calling me? What were the plans now? Would I be forever confined to my bedroom and never have a normal life again? Had Donnie simply returned to his normal life and left me behind?* I had no answers. I was a living zombie.

I felt as if I was living in an out-of-body experience. I could picture and see everything around me that was happening, but this could not possibly be my life. For the next few days or so, it seemed as if life just simply went on as before. Everyone appeared to have returned to their normal day-to-day functions except for me. My parents went to the store each morning as usual. My siblings spent their days doing whatever. I would get up and make breakfast as I would if I were going to school. I would help my siblings get prepared for their day. When everyone left, there I was … standing in the house alone. I had no idea what was happening around me. I had no idea how anyone felt about things or about me. I had no idea where Donnie was.

I tried to live in denial, but it was impossible. The real humiliation and embarrassment of this situation hit me with full force. I was not in this world alone. *What did my younger sisters think of me? Did they think I was a slut? Did they even know what was going on? Were they old enough to understand? What about my younger brother and my older brothers? Is anyone ever going to love me or look at me the same again? Is this what people … other people … mature adults … do when they get pregnant?*

On top of all the mental anguish I was putting myself through trying to sort things out, my body was changing rapidly in ways I did not understand. *Was anyone ever going to simply sit me down and try to help me understand all of this? Was I going to have the baby but never get married? Would I ever see Donnie again? If I did have the baby, was Donnie going to be an active part of its life? Were Donnie's parents going to accept this child as their grandchild? Was I ever going back to school and have a normal life? What did my friends think of me, or did they even know what was going on?*

Finally, the silence was broken. One morning before I got up to help with the children and fix breakfast, my mom came to my room. She simply told me to get showered and dressed, with no other explanation. I felt like I was an outsider living in a house of strangers. I was in prison in my own home. I was simply going through the motions of life and doing as I was instructed to do.

I did not see a lot of my dad, not that I did anyway, but it just seemed like he disappeared. I knew he was around because late at night, when he returned home from the store, he would slip into my room and kiss me goodnight when he thought I was asleep. How many nights I just wanted to reach up and hug him and say I was sorry. I would have given anything to feel his strong arms around me and hear him say that everything would be ok … that he loved me just as much as he ever did … that I was still his little girl. I didn't, and he didn't. *Daddy, do you still love me?*

I got up and showered as I was instructed. When I came out of my bedroom, dressed and ready for whatever lay ahead, my mom got her purse and we left the house. We drove into town to a doctor's office. We did not speak at any time during the trip, in the doctor's office, or on the way home. When my name was called, my mom got up with me and we followed the nurse to one of the back rooms. Going down the hallway to his office, on both sides of me plastered all over the walls, were pictures of babies. Babies smiling ... babies being fed ... babies being cuddled by their moms! Babies everywhere. Would a picture of my baby ever make it to the wall? I somehow doubted it.

My mom told the doctor I was having a lot of issues because I was under so much stress. *Is that what I am going through … stress?* I was not sure what she was referring to, but I simply listened. The doctor instructed me to sit on the bed and he gave me a shot. He explained to me that the shot would alleviate some of my discomfort and help me relax. *What discomfort?* The only discomfort I felt was in my heart and not as a direct result of the pregnancy. I could not imagine any shot he gave me would alleviate my mental anguish, but if he said it was so, then I guess it was just another thing I simply did not understand. They were the adults and obviously they knew better than me.

On the return trip back to the house, my mother did not say anything until we got almost home. She then advised me I needed to write a letter outlining why I felt I could not have this baby. *Did I say I could not have this baby? What in the world is she talking about?* Again, I should have asked these questions, but I did not. Donnie should have been here to ask these questions, but he wasn't! *Am I losing my mind?* We arrived at the house. When we went in, my mom again instructed me about the letter and she advised me I needed to do this now. In my mind, I could not figure out how all this related to me being pregnant or what the importance of it all was.

Before I even knew what was happening, I was writing a letter one day outlining all the reasons I should not have this baby. I had to write this letter for a judge, a doctor, or someone. It was a requirement. *A requirement of what? Would someone simply explain to me what is happening?* I was scared to death. I did not know what to do. I had absolutely no one to talk to. *Would I always feel this alienated the remainder of my life? What about my baby? Who was going to raise it? What in the world is happening here!!!!????*

By events and whisperings which I overheard, I think I now had figured out that the wheels had been put into motion for me to enter the hospital and terminate the pregnancy. Though I never said this out loud, I felt it in the pit of my gut. Abortions were done in those days, but they were not as simple as they are today. I could not just go to the doctor and end it. There was red tape that had to be completed, and this letter from me, I think, was the starting point. *Did I ever question what was going on?* No. I simply followed instructions. *Was it ever discussed with me?* No. *Was it ever discussed with Donnie?* I do not know. *Did my older brother who was Donnie's friend know what was going on and share it with Donnie?* I do not know. As close as my brother and I were … and believe me, we were closer than a brother and sister ever were … not even he and I discussed this. Whatever was happening had to be leading to a solution, but what the solution was I was not clued in. I knew but I did not want to know. *Does that make sense to you?* Please remember that my world, up to this point, was my boyfriend and school. Sure, I had a lot of personal responsibilities in my life, but I was fine. It could have been worse. I could be getting into trouble with the law as some family members were. I could be sneaking to do drugs as some of my friends were. No, I was just pregnant and alone. Alone as I had never been before in my life and alone as I never wanted to be again. I made the promise to myself that if I ever got through this, I would never allow anyone to hurt me again or dictate my life to me.

I wrote the letter stating what I knew I was to say. *Was it rehearsed with me?* No! I just knew what my life plan was supposed to be. I had heard it day in and day out throughout the years. I knew this was what I needed to write. I knew I had to share what this pregnancy was doing to my family. I had to outline how it was such a disgrace, and how having this baby would affect the lives of all those around me. But worse than that, I knew I had to write it in a way that would make it my words and not the thoughts of others. I had to convince whoever was receiving this letter that this was my decision, and nobody had coerced me. No one did coerce me ... I just knew what I was to say! I wrote the letter and I must have done it well because a few days later I was in a hospital room having an abortion.

I say I was having an abortion, but at the time I was not sure. I just know that sometime during the night I awoke at home with this pain in my stomach. I thought at first it might have been something I ate, but then I could not remember whether I had even eaten. I do not think I ate that day at all. I remember just lying there thinking it would go away. As time slipped by, the pain increased. Finally, I had no choice but to wake my parents. I was in such agony and I thought I was dying. Something horrible was wrong with me and I was scared.

I managed to get out of bed, go around the corner, and enter my parents' bedroom. They must have heard me moving around before I came to them because by the time I turned on their bedroom light and got to their bed to wake them, they were already out of bed and were getting dressed. My mother took me back to my bedroom and helped me get my clothes on. You could see fear written all over her face. I could tell she was struggling with holding back tears. When I had finished getting ready, she embraced me in a way she never had before. I could feel all her fear. I could sense how much she truly loved me. She only wanted what was best for me. I had understood that all along. We may not have spoken those feelings to each other, but I knew it. My parents may not have been perfect, but they did one thing with perfection … love us! As she let go of me, she asked me to hurry and come in the living room as soon as I could. Before I knew it, they were rushing me out the front door.

I was so confused. I did not understand exactly what was happening. *Why are my parents in such a hurry? Why not just give me something to take the pain away? Have they called the doctor and he said to bring me in? Could the doctor not give me another shot to ease my pain as he did with the shot for anxiety?* I did not see my parents on the telephone, but maybe my dad called while my mom was helping me get ready. This would be so much easier if someone would just talk to me.

I crawled in the back seat of the car. My dad drove. My mom rode in the back with me. She simply held me. Eventually she could no longer hold back the tears. I wanted so desperately to console her, but I couldn't. I was the one causing her this pain. *What could I possibly say now to make her feel better?* My mind was going in all sorts of directions. *Who was taking care of my younger siblings? Am I even awake?* Yes, I have to be awake, and this has to be real because the pain I am feeling is no dream. It seemed like forever that we were in the car, but we finally arrived at the hospital. My dad drove the car right up to the emergency room door. My mom got out while we waited in the car. Shortly afterwards, she returned with a nurse and a gurney. I got out of the car, got on top of the gurney, and I was rolled into the hospital. Still no explanations as to what was happening. By now I really did not care to understand. I simply wanted something for the pain. The pain was all consuming and I could not think of anything else.

I wish I could say to you I simply went to the hospital and shortly thereafter everything was fine. I wish I could say to you I truly understood what was going on around me, but I did not. I wish I could say it was painless, both mentally and physically, but it was not. This moment in time would be forever etched in my memory bank and it would affect my life for years and years to come. I would bury it and go on, but it would rear its ugly head in many, many ways throughout my teen and adult life. It would affect my first marriage. It would affect my relationships with my younger sisters. It would forever put a wall between me and my parents, especially my mom and me. It would affect my younger brother in ways I would never learn until recently. But it was what had to occur to remedy the situation and that is what mattered, *right?*

I was checked in at the hospital. I was put in a hospital gown and placed in a room by myself. I was hooked up to some fluids and the nightmare continued. Remember, by this time, I was at least 3 months pregnant. This life inside of me had limbs and was as much a human being as you and I. *Did I think of this?* I did not think of anything. I simply suffered and thought my life was on the verge of ending. I had to be dying. What else could possibly hurt this badly?

I was given another shot at the hospital and I thought it was to help alleviate the pain. Shortly after the shot, my body did all sorts of weird things. The nurse would remain in the room with me, but the doctor would only come in periodically to check on me. My mom and dad would rotate being in the room. Because I was so far along in my pregnancy, I was going through labor though I did not realize it at first. I was 15 years old, and I had never had much physical pain in my life. I just wanted to die so the pain would cease, and this would be over. It went on forever, so it seemed. It did, however, go on for over fifteen hours.

My parents continued to rotate coming in and out of the room to check on me, but you could see the pain in their eyes and feel the hurt in their hearts. They could only manage to stay a short period of time. It was tearing them apart. For the first time in my life, I would see my dad cry. He would get angry at the doctors and demand they give me something for pain. He would pace back and forth. He had so much anger in his eyes it scared me. I had never seen my daddy angry with me at all, much less in this way. I soon discovered the anger was not directed at me. The tears were for me.

Between the bouts of pain when I could think again, I was thinking of Donnie. *Did he know anything about this?* I did remember when we left the house for the hospital that morning, my brother left for work as normal. He would join Donnie at work like any other day, but today he would tell Donnie I had to be taken to the hospital because I was having problems with my pregnancy. It was what he was told to tell Donnie, and he did. What my parents did not anticipate happening was Donnie leaving work and coming to the hospital. My brother would come with him, but he would never get out of the car.

I can remember hearing loud voices outside my hospital room. I would have known that voice anywhere ... *it was Donnie!* I knew it was Donnie, but I was in too much pain to be able to do anything. If I could just holler his name so he would know where to find me! I opened my mouth but nothing! My pain prevented me from doing anything except balling up in a fetal position and crying. Eventually I knew my dad had forbid Donnie entry into the room. The anger from my dad that I mentioned earlier was evident in his tone when speaking outside of my room. I would not see Donnie during any of this.

When the birth was over, I heard my mom gasp and say, *"It's a boy"*. I never saw my son. I do not even know what they did with him. Two days later I would leave the hospital and life was supposed to return to normal.

Chapter Twelve

My summer was long and miserable. I returned to school in August not knowing what anyone knew. I could not focus. I could not think of anything but what had happened to me. I could not get the words that my mother had said out of my head … *it is a boy!* I had a son and I never got to hold him, look at him, or kiss his tiny face. James Michael, the name I had picked out earlier, was gone. I was a mother. *How am I supposed to act? What am I supposed to do with that information*? I had no answers to any of the questions swirling around in my head, but I did know one thing for sure. I was not the same person I was before. Though I was 15 in numbers, I felt all grown up. I did not want to laugh or have fun anymore. I went through the motions of living, but I did not know where I fit in.

I remember one day sitting in my room on the bed. I was looking around at everything I had, especially all the ribbons and trophies that Donnie had won in horseshows. They were plastered all over my walls and on my shelves. I conjured up in my mind what our son would have looked like. As I put my face together with Donnie's, I tried to picture what James Michael would look like. *Would he have my eyes or his dad's? Would he have my big nose … oh gosh, I would hope not! Did he look like me or like Donnie?* I would never have answers to these questions. I got up and circled January 15th on my calendar hanging in my room. This was the due date the doctor who confirmed my pregnancy had given me. It was a day I would remember every year for the remainder of my life. I did not just have an abortion. I was physically aching for the loss of my son. *How does a 15-year-old do that*? I do not know, but I did. I would continue to ache for him every day of my life, especially on January 15th of each year to come.

Never again would this situation be spoken of in our home. I continued with my schooling and life went on. I was forbidden to ever see Donnie again, but this one thing my parents would not be able to control. Donnie refused to stop dating me. Because of his determination, it gave me courage to stand up to my parents also. I was no longer a young girl who could be controlled. My parents knew this, and they finally relented because they had no choice. It would never be the same between any of us. *How could it be?* Whenever Donnie entered the house and my dad was there, my dad would exit out another door. *How could I possibly be happy like this?* The two most important men in my life could not stand to be in the same room together. *How was this even going to work?* The one thing I did have clear understanding of was that I could not lose Donnie now. Our love was stronger, and we would go on with our plans as if this never took place. *Did we talk about what had happened? Never!* Not once did we ever discuss what happened to me at the hospital, or the real reasons I was there.

As much as we loved one another, Donnie and I would soon learn things could never be the same between us. I felt as if our relationship was like everything that led up to this point … we were simply going through the motions in our relationship. Were we really in love now or just determined to get back at our parents and show them we were in control? No, we were in love, but it was no longer the fun, carefree love it should have been or that it once was. We were growing apart though we were still together. Donnie was shutting me out more and more, and he was dating other girls behind my back. I did not seem to have any say over anything pertaining to our relationship. He did continually remind me he loved me, and I believed him. He always came back. I also loved him too much to let go.

Time would pass but the pain never would. The memory of it would stay with me every moment of every day. I knew I had to let it go or I would never move on, so I buried it so deep that I convinced myself it never happened. Donnie and I were continually fighting. I was surprised we managed to attend my Junior prom together, but we did. We hung in there. Summer came and went. I was starting my Senior year and life was moving forward. Shortly thereafter, Donnie and I would finally have a major blow up ... *the final blow up* ... and we would go our separate ways. I told myself I did not care. We had caused each other enough pain, and it was time to realize it was over.

After a month or so of being broke up, Donnie's mom called me one evening. It was raining outside, and I can still hear the desperation in her voice. It was September of 1974. I don't remember the exact day. His mom called to advise me that Donnie had joined the Army. He was in Richmond waiting to be shipped out to basic training camp. She had not known until he called her. It seemed he did not tell anyone what his plans were. He had called his mom and requested she call me. I could not believe what she was telling me. *Why in the world would he do such a thing?* I pulled myself together and drove to Donnie's parent's house. I picked his mother up and we headed to Richmond to see Donnie before his flight left. It was the longest drive of my life for many reasons ... the weather, the desire to see Donnie, and the fact that his mom and I never said two words during the whole drive. This was the first time we had seen each other since the day we were at the courthouse trying to get a marriage license. *Had it really been an eternity since that happened?* I am sure I was the last person she wanted to be making this trip with. I wanted to discuss our past situation with her, but I could never get the words out of my mouth. I was too afraid to hear what I was sure she wanted to say to me. It was best left unsaid.

We finally located the motel Donnie was at and we spent as much time with him as we could before he had to leave. Now the good-byes had to be said. His mother returned to the car to give us some time alone. I can remember it just as though it happened yesterday. We were standing outside under an awning in the rain. We could not kiss each other enough and we were both crying. We made all the promises a young couple would in those circumstances, and I am sure we meant them all. *Did we talk about why he did this?* No. We had lost the ability to communicate honestly in all this mess, but we did not lose the love we felt for each other. I realized at that moment that I loved him more than I ever did, if that was even possible. I would wait for him no matter how long it took, and I knew he felt the same. How naïve young hearts can be!

Donnie was gone and with him went my sense of security. I could ignore all the things I felt I lacked in my life before because Donnie made it all seem fine. He gave me all the love and affection that I needed. He provided for me all the things I lacked at home. He gave me the desire to be the best I could and not get off course. He inspired me not to do all the things other kids were doing at my age. He was my world, and now it was no longer. I reckoned it would all work out though because we loved each other, and I would just be content with the letters, the periodic telephone calls, and the home visits that were so few and far between. ***Wrong!***

My Senior year was full of everything except what I truly needed. My anger and hurt over the past had changed me in big ways. I no longer seemed to care what I did, who I did it too, or the consequences. I made some major mistakes that year which would cost me dearly, especially in the loss of two very dear and special friends. I did something which was unforgivable in more ways than one. I denied it, of course, but it was no use. My actions revealed all they needed to know, which was that I had done just what they accused me of doing. Again, as with all things in life, the consequences far outweighed the crime. I have had a void in my heart ever since for these friends. I would see them periodically over the years and make attempts at restoring what I had lost. It never was or ever could be the same.

When Donnie came home for his first leave, we were both very nervous with one another. We were so happy and excited to see each other, but there was a void we could not deny. We spent his final day at home with his parents. In the back of this book, you will find a picture we took together in his mom's kitchen. It would be our last picture as a military couple.

When Donnie's parents and I took him to the airport to catch his plane back to the Army, I remember waving good bye to him with tears in my eyes. I knew it would be our last good bye. Nothing really occurred, but I just sensed it in my heart. His dad must have felt it too. Donnie's dad was not an affectionate person. However, on this day, his dad came up beside me, put his arm around me, and said, "Don't worry, he will be back!" I thought to myself, "Yes, he will but he will not be returning to me." I never said it out loud, but I knew it to be true.

Donnie joined the Army during a very important time in my life. What should have been proms and fun turned out to be loneliness. I was just beginning my senior year in school, and it should have been an exciting time for me. It was anything but exciting. Girls were planning for their prom, but what about me? My boyfriend was worlds away. I could not go to the prom. To make matters worse, I knew Donnie was writing other girls. One girl that caused us a lot of strife was spending time at Donnie's house with his mom, sharing with her the letters she received from Donnie. *How did I know?* I lived in a small town. Donnie's family was more than happy to let me know what was going on. I was no longer good enough for Donnie, and they did not hide the fact that they felt this way.

A family member offered to take me to the prom, but what was the use? I could not imagine going with anyone but Donnie. I spent my senior year in turmoil. I had been to my junior prom with Donnie last year, but I would not attend my senior prom. My grades would start to slip, and life would start to spiral out of control even more.

Donnie would call me like clockwork almost every weekend, but it was not enough. I missed him so much I hurt. I think he could feel our relationship slipping away too. In what I perceived as a desperate attempt at keeping us together, Donnie asked me to marry him. He said he would make the arrangements and we could be married the next weekend he came home. I could get on board with that. I shared this with my parents, and to my surprise, they did not try to discourage it. My mother took me to purchase a dress to wear, and we were sharing in a way we had not done in a very long time. We laughed together. We cried together. We planned my marriage weekend together. The church was rented. The dress was purchased. No one would be present but our families ... or at least mine ... and I was so happy. Finally, Donnie and I would be together. It was a bit scary to know I would leave my family and join Donnie where he was, but I was willing to make that sacrifice. You had to understand that though my family was as dysfunctional as they were, I loved them very much. I could not imagine my life without them or being so far away from them. Regardless, it would all work out because I would be with Donnie.

The weekend we set aside to get married was fast approaching and I was as nervous as I could be. I went to school on Friday. Donnie was going to fly in on Saturday. We would be married on Saturday afternoon. My mom had even purchased a small white Bible for me to carry when I walked down the aisle. It was not the wedding I had always dreamed about, but those days were long gone. I was no longer that unscathed innocent girl. I just wanted to get married and start my life with Donnie. My parents never mentioned college any longer. I guess they had long given up on their dreams for me as well. What I had put them through was too much hurt for them and they gave up on all the dreams they once had for me.

When Saturday morning finally arrived, I had to run some errands. I cannot remember what they were, but I do remember I was away from the house that morning. When I returned, a family member met me at the door and said that Donnie had been trying to call me all morning. They said they did not know what was going on, but they suspected by the tone of Donnie's voice that it was not good.

Shortly after that Donnie called once again. He told me that his Sergeant in the Army would not give him leave to come home. The wedding would not happen. I was simply devastated. After we hung up, I knew things would never be the same. I was so hurt and angry. I could feel something inside of me die.

Donnie and I would not make it as a couple. I really did not care by now. After graduation, I was free. I began to party as much as possible. I drank more than most girls my age and I did not care what Donnie did or who he did it with. My parents had no control over me. My relationship with my mother deteriorated, but my relationship with my dad, in some ways, became my safe-haven. He did not try to make me stop partying and drinking, but if I needed him to come to my rescue, he would. I think he was afraid of losing me and my mom was just angry at it all. It brought more torment into their marriage and they did not need any more turmoil in their lives than they already had. Other family members were constantly in trouble or involved with drugs or whatever, and they did not need me adding to their heartache. I did not care. I think deep down inside I thought they deserved it, but in my heart, I felt so guilty for what they were going through. As we all do when we are the ones hurting, we become very self-centered and think only of ourselves. It is so true that hurting people, hurt people!

Though my life was a complete mess by most standards, I was having fun and enjoying life. I had two male friends I loved dearly, and I felt truly blessed to have them in my life. I had gone to school with them both, but when in school, we never really associated. It was after graduation that we truly bonded and became close. We were practically inseparable. At times, they truly were my light in the darkness.

They partied with me. They cared for me. They watched out for me. They were my knights in shining armor. When we each had dates, we would all plan to meet up afterwards and hang out. They were a large part of my daily existence. Eventually, however, as with all things in my life at this time, I lost them too. As would be expected, they found girls they wanted to spend their lives with. For whatever reason, I was eliminated from this stage of their lives. I never could understand why they felt they had to let me go to move forward. I thought we were best friends and always would be. They left a forever void in my heart. About this same time, I also had a male friend who was much older than me. He was married and had daughters my age. Our relationship was purely platonic, but people tried to make it ugly and speculate that they knew more than they did. He would remain my forever friend for many, many years. No matter where I was in life, I could pick up the telephone and call him. He was forever coming to my rescue. He is still living today though he has to be in his late 80's. I think of him often, and I pray for him and his family. I have not communicated with him in probably twenty years or more.

In late 1977, one day while I was at home a friend came over. She brought with her news that would shake me to the very core of my being, if that was possible. Everything I had endured up to this point in my life had made me hard on the inside. Not hard enough though to prepare me for what she had to say. She advised me Donnie had gotten married to a girl in Germany and it was in the local paper. I thought I would die inside, but on the outside, I was tough as nails. No more hurting for me. I know I cried a bit in front of her and my mom, but it was nothing compared to what I was feeling inside. As I was crying, I remembered a letter I had received from Donnie just about a month ago. I did not understand what he was talking about at the time, but now it all made sense. I will not share the contents of that letter out of respect for many people, but I knew without a doubt it would never be over for us. We had not communicated in a long time, so his letter took me by surprise. When I received it, I put it down and never gave it another thought. I often wondered if he wanted to hurt me for what he thought I had done to him. How pitiful a person I had become! How horrible I felt because I told myself I had basically given away the only person I ever loved as I loved him.

At this point, I want to interject that Donnie married a wonderful lady from Germany and they went on to have four children. I do not ever want to take away from that relationship. I do not know his ex-wife personally, but I have had occasion to meet her. She must be a wonderful person for Donnie to choose her. Nothing that occurred between Donnie and I was her fault. She was the best mother and wife he could have asked for. It is the two of us that should feel ashamed. I struggled with self-loathing for many years because of the hurt I may have caused others. I know now I have to forgive myself as God has forgiven me. This book and this testimony is my way of using the horrible things in my life to hopefully help someone else not make the same mistakes. Donnie loved his wife very much, but as was the same with me, in his mind I was only a thought away.

I made the comment above that Donnie may have wanted to hurt me for what I had done to him. Sometime before he got married, I started dating Donnie's best friend. Yes, I did do it for spite. I did not realize it at the time, but now, as I look back, I know what my intentions were. I feel horrible even admitting this, but if I want to glorify Christ in my life, then I must be honest about where He brought me from. I was not a nice person in so many ways. Donnie's best friend was a wonderful person. He loved me, and I cared about him a great deal. I would go so far as to say I loved him, but as we can see up until this point, I had no idea what love was. I just know I hurt him. I just praise God that he would go on to marry a girl who truly loved him. This man went through a horrible incident and it left him disabled in many ways. His wife has stood beside him all the way, and it fills my heart with comfort to know that she has. Again, I do not personally know his wife, but she had to be of impeccable character to honor her role as his wife all these years. She not only stood by him, but she also raised his children who were young when he was injured. I have told God many times how I wish I had the forgiveness of Donnie's wife or his best friend's wife. They both are remarkable women from what I know of them. I only wish I could measure up to be the women they are. In those days, I was anything but honorable. Both these men were truly blessed to have these wonderful ladies as their partners for life.

Over the course of time, I would see Donnie totally out of the blue. Once when I returned from Texas, I saw Donnie at a distance as soon as I arrived home. The second time I saw Donnie I was with my husband. We were travelling, and we got off at an exit two hours from home to purchase gas. As we entered the gas station, I glanced around at a truck I saw. What made it weird was that I thought I saw Donnie in the truck. Of course, this could not be as we were nowhere near where Donnie or his family lived. As we got closer, I realized it was indeed Donnie, along with his wife and their young son. Irony would do things like this to me over the years. It was as if life was pointing a finger at me and taunting me.

By this time, my parents had sold their grocery store and had a restaurant. I was living on my own but working part-time with my dad at the restaurant. Hanging on the wall over the counter was a big picture of my graduation. I guess my parents were proud I even got so far as to graduate considering my life up until that point. My mom shared with me how one day as she was coming out of the kitchen towards the counter, she noticed a soldier sitting there in his uniform just staring up at my picture. She soon realized that the soldier was Donnie. He simply stopped in to say hello. I guess he felt he could. My mom shared that she chatted with him for a bit and then he left.

Chapter Thirteen

You would think that based on what I have shared up until now, Donnie and I would have finally severed all ties and gone separate ways. *Was it over for us?* No! I am not sure it ever would be. We were not capable of leaving one another alone. We felt robbed by others. I think we both carried a lot of bitterness on the inside because of what we did to each other and what was done to us by others.

Years would pass. I would graduate from high school. I would go to college. I would get married. *Did I ever stop loving Donnie?* No, I did not. I just buried it in that safe place with everything else I have buried, and I would go on. I entered into a totally different world, and the roads I traveled would not be the ones that were planned for me.

Donnie was gone, and I was angry. I did not realize I was angry, but I was. I started hanging out with the party crowd, and the nice life my parents planned for me was out the window. All I wanted to do after Donnie left was get rid of the pain. I would learn to seek security in other ways … in partying … in drinking … and gradually in marriage. My future husband and I got married in 1980 after living together for two years. I was 22 at the time. I loved my husband to the best of my ability, but what I had been taught love was up to this point by past relationships was not what it should have been. I gave my husband the best there was left to give. I just could not give him all of me. There was a part of my heart that would never be able to let go of Donnie.

My husband was a good man … hard working … provided well for me … did whatever I wanted … was good looking … and best of all, my parents and family loved him. His family was good to me, but his mom, in the beginning, was not very warm towards me. There was a lot of strife between his mom and me, but over the course of time, I came to love her very much and I know she felt the same.

My husband and I met in a bar. Right from the beginning, we had a common interest and that was partying. We loved to party, and we did it well.

Prior to our marriage and while we were living together, an opportunity presented itself for us to adopt a 5-year-old girl who was being raised by my parents. She was biologically the daughter of my half-sister. It was a long and complicated story, but things were not going well in my family. My mom's health had deteriorated over the years, and my parents were getting up in age. Though this little girl had been living with them for almost 3 years as their daughter, things had happened that prevented her from continuing in this role. Feeling personally responsible for the well-being of my family as I did, my husband and I agreed to raise her as our daughter. I had to do this because my parents were hurting so much. They loved this child so much and the thought of losing her completely would have been more than they could have taken. I could not and would not allow this to hurt my parents even more than their children had already hurt them thus far.

What did I know about being a mother? As far as I was concerned, I did not deserve to be a mother. I had the chance once and I killed it, literally. I blamed myself for losing the only child I truly loved and now I was trying to make it up with someone else's child. I was not stable enough in my life to be a good role model, but again, I felt responsible for the child as well. She was part of our family and, as such, she was my responsibility whether she truly was or not. During her years with my parents, I grew to love her as if she had always been a part of us. I could not allow her to be hurt more than she had already been. She was only five years of age. She had already endured so much. I felt she deserved to be loved, and I so wanted to love her. I already loved her immensely as a family member, but now I wanted to love her as a daughter.

Just like that, we became parents. It was this situation that nudged us to get married. I know that sounds unfair to all of us and it probably was. A part of me was truly excited about being a mom and a wife, but the other side of me … the part that I listened to the most … well that part could not admit any of the feelings I was going through. I could not afford to care. Look where it had gotten me so far in life!

This child would be a true blessing to me even if I did not realize it at the time. It was a very difficult time for her. It was even more difficult for us to bond as mother and daughter. Basically, she had a lot of issues of her own and I was an emotional wreck. We did not have a lot going for us in the relationship department. She had grown to love my mother so much and I would always be jealous of how she felt towards my mom. I always felt second best when in the presence of my mom and my daughter. I was a wounded young girl trying to be a mature mother. How could this possibly be? I was clueless as to how to love a child. Add this to all the buried anger and hurt on the inside of me and you have a disaster on your hands. As much as I loved my mother, I resented her. It was a constant emotional tug of war for me on the inside, but you can bet one thing … I never showed it on the outside!

However, and I want to make this abundantly clear, this little girl became my daughter and I could not love her more if I had given birth to her. We have a very healthy and well-balanced relationship today. I am very proud of the woman she has become. She has blessed me with three beautiful grandchildren. She would bring more to my life than I ever gave.

As the years passed, I decided I wanted to have a child of my own. We already had our daughter, but it was not the same. I wanted a child who was an extension of me. I physically yearned in my soul for an infant ... *to see that precious child reach its arms out to me ... to hear the first time it would call me mom ... to feel it grow on the inside of me ... to know someone out there was truly a part of me ... to smell that odor which only an infant has.* I yearned inside and physically ached for a baby of my own!

My husband, on the other hand, did not seem to care one way or the other. We had been married for five years now and lived about three hours from my family. I was far from ready to have a child mentally, but I thought it was time and so did both our families. I was so insecure and realize now that I wanted a child to complete me. I felt less than a woman without a child, and I needed someone to just love me unconditionally. I needed to feel I was irreplaceable in the life of someone. I knew I was important to my family, but it was not enough. I knew my husband loved me. He was wonderful to me. I just yearned so desperately for a child to call my own. My husband never understood me. We had loads of fun together, but we never had the trust or ability to communicate that we should have had.

Why I had not conceived by now was a mystery because we never used contraceptives when we were intimate. I had never in my life used contraceptives so why now? After my abortion, the doctor put me on birth control pills to help regulate my monthly cycles. I suffered so much during those times and the birth control pills supposedly would help alleviate some of the pain. However, after trying every birth control pill on the market, I had to cease taking them because I would simply get sick. I chose to use nothing.

I should have realized over the years something was wrong. If I were completely honest with myself, I probably did. As always, I did not want to think about it, so I buried the idea of anything wrong deep in that safe place where I kept storing all hurts in life I did not want to deal with. It had always worked before. *Let's not dwell on reality but continue to live in my hurt-free made up world.* When I want to get pregnant, it will happen. I kept reasoning with myself that because I had gotten pregnant early in life, then that was a definite indicator I would get pregnant again.

Pretty stupid thinking for a 27-year-old, huh? Not stupid … simply uneducated. I never was taught to go for yearly checkups, and I do not think I had been back to an OB/GYN since my abortion. How many years ago had that been? Oh well, it did not matter. I will worry about it later.

At some point in life, we need to accept responsibility for our decisions in life. Not me … I wanted to continue to blame others for what was wrong in my life. Not going to an OB/GYN had never been something I did, but shouldn't I have been mature enough by now to have figured this out? You'd think!

At some point during this process, we made a definitive decision to move forward with starting our own family. I went to a doctor, passed the physical, and everything seemed fine. The fact that I had not yet conceived before now did not seem such a big deal and it was explained away. I was excited.

Months and months would pass, and nothing would happen. I would go back to the doctor and they would again reassure us everything appeared fine. Finally, they could not deny that something was amiss. After a while, they decided to check my husband to make sure he was healthy. We did, and he was. *So, what was wrong?* Nothing was wrong. We were just stressing too much, or at least I was. This is how they explained everything away.

I think by now my husband was just going through the motions to keep me happy. I am not sure he did not want children as much as he simply did not care. He already had a son by a previous marriage. He was not involved in the child's life for many reasons, but it only made me more intent on having a child. Everyone else seemed to have one and I wanted one. I would act as if I did not care to protect myself. I did care, however, and it was becoming an obsession with me. My daughter was getting older and I wanted a child while she was still young enough to enjoy a brother or sister. On top of that, I was getting scared and the anger I was hiding so well was just increasing and increasing. It was like a pot in the pit of my gut which was set on simmer. At some point in life, it would boil over. How could it not?

As much as I did not want to remember what occurred when I was younger, I could not help but think about it. *What if the child I murdered would be my only birth child? What if the decision my parents made for me cost me future children?*

Donnie was married now and had several children. Was I the only one to be punished for the mistake we made together? Close friends I had in high school had abortions also. They had children now so why could I not have any? *Oh forget it!* Bury all these thoughts even deeper because I knew that someday I would have a child of my own. I had to. I could not fail my parents yet again and prove to be a failure at this too.

To make matters even worse, both of my younger sisters were married now. By this time, my mother was running a gift shop in town. One weekend when I was home visiting, I was at the shop with mom. Before I left to head back to my parents' home, one of my younger sisters and her new husband returned from vacation. She looked so happy and seemed to have this special glow about her on this day, but why wouldn't she? She and her husband were still newlyweds. As I walked out of the shop to get in my truck, she followed me outside. I opened my truck door on the driver's side and slid in. As I went to shut the driver's door, my sister stepped between the door and me. She stooped down so we were at eye level with one another. She looked fearful as she handed me a gift. As she gave me the gift, I thought she had tears in her eyes. She said, *"Before you open this know that I love you so much".* I was at a total loss as to what was going on, so I opened the gift. It was a coffee mug that read, *"The World's Greatest God Mother".* I looked at the mug and then at her. I knew what it meant, but I did not want to acknowledge it or verbalize it. I am not sure I could have at that precise moment. Before I could say a word, she said, *"Please tell me you are happy for me".* I started to cry, and we just sat there hugging one another. Words did not need to be spoken because I knew she was pregnant. As happy as I was for her because I loved her so much, deep in the pit of my gut I could feel the anger expanding yet again. As was the norm for me, I ignored it and told her how happy I was for her. *Again, I lied!* I was happy for her, but I also was very angry.

I left the shop and I cried all the way to my mom's house. I could feel the anger inside of me wanting to explode and I wanted to just scream. *How could this be happening?* I was the older sister. I should have been the one to have children first. This should have been my moment in the sun and I was robbed of it. I hated my sister as much as I loved her. I hated Donnie all over again. I hated my parents. I hated everyone. I especially hated God, if He truly existed. If He was all that my sister tried to tell me He was, then why was He allowing this to happen to me? I did not want to hear about a God that put me through all of this. I was convinced He was punishing me for what I did. I just wondered how long it would continue. As always, I had to keep this to myself. How selfish of me would it be to inflict all this anger on others? This was something I needed to deal with on my own. I did not even discuss it with my husband.

Life continued as normally as it could for me. Then one day I would learn Donnie was back in the states. He was stationed a few hours from where I lived, with his wife and children. You would think this would have little effect on me, or at least the effect would be minimal, but it was not. All the love I felt for him as a teenager returned, and I was back in time. I had to see him, and I would do whatever I needed to make it happen. The fact that I was a married woman now with a daughter, and he was a married man with children, should have meant something to me. But it did not. I was too in love and I deserved to see him. It was our parent's fault we were not together. I had to see if he still loved me. I should have been married to him. I should have been the one to give him children. *With thoughts running through my mind like these, is it any wonder I was incapable of thinking of others?*

You have to realize that seeing Donnie did not register as infidelity in my screwed up mind. I reasoned it out as my privilege ... it was something I was entitled to. The thought I was being unfaithful to my husband never once entered my thoughts. Donnie was the first in my life and that entitled me to more than it should have, or so I reasoned. I cannot say it enough ... how selfish an individual I was at that time in my life! Not long afterwards, I heard Donnie was again transferred overseas.

My husband knew about Donnie from my family and photos. He also knew about him from a box of letters he found shortly after we were married. He made me destroy all of them. I can remember the day I did. I was on our bed in our home crying. I must have had a hundred letters or so. They were thrown all over the bed. I sat there and read every one of them before I destroyed them. I also came across an 8x10 photo of Donnie in his service uniform that I had kept. It was still in the frame. On the bottom right corner of the picture, there was a leaf with writing on it. It was a leaf Donnie had picked up during one of his times out in the field performing what the Army referred to as "War Games". While he was out there, he was thinking of me, so he picked up the leaf and wrote on it, *"To my one and only ... I love and miss you!"* He sent it to me. This is how much we loved one another. How could we simply let that go?

There was another time Donnie sent me a cassette of him playing the guitar and singing. He had made this cassette especially for me while outside his barracks one evening. He said his heart was heavy from missing me. He sang "My

Sweet Lady" by John Denver and "Fraulein". I kept it all as close as I could, but like Donnie, they would soon be gone too.

After reading all the letters and tearing them up, I wiped my eyes and got up as if nothing had happened. I was so good at denial. It truly was one of my many character traits I did so well. My husband and I never discussed the letters or Donnie again. I thought to myself that people could destroy the evidence that Donnie and I ever existed, but they could never destroy my memories and how I felt.

Chapter Fourteen

My husband and I decided to move closer to my family in Gordonsville, Virginia. I had told him when we married that I would remain in Chesapeake long enough for him to put in ten years at his job, and then I wanted to go home. I needed my family near me as I struggled with the issue of having children. Besides, my parents needed me. They were going through so much in their own lives, and I felt so guilty all the time because I was three hours away. I tried to get home at least every other weekend, but it was not enough … not for me or for them.

When we shared with my parents the idea we were moving home, they appeared to be happy. I would learn later that my mom advised my husband that it was not a good idea to bring me so close to where Donnie would someday return. Obviously, my mom understood more than I gave her credit for or that she shared with me. She knew where part of my heart was even if I did not. I had convinced myself I was happy in my marriage and moving home would not be detrimental to our relationship. Just as I never did, my husband did not listen to my mom's advice. We moved.

When my husband and I got married, though we were living in Chesapeake, Virginia, we had our ceremony at a church in Gordonsville, Virginia. I wanted to get married in familiar territory, but mostly I wanted to have it there to make things easier on my parents. By this time in their lives, they had suffered some financial setbacks and could not afford to pay for my wedding. We paid for it ourselves. My mom made all the flowers because she was the best flower maker around.

At the reception after our wedding, I was speaking with one of my girlfriends. She told me that on her way to my wedding she saw Donnie. *How ironic was that*? As I said, irony was always pointing its finger at me and laughing. Immediately I thought to myself, *"maybe this is a sign that I was not to get married"*. It did not matter. I was now someone else's wife. I truly thought I could honor my vows. I did love my husband in my own special way. He made me laugh and we had fun. We truly were the ideal couple in so many ways. We wrestled together ... we partied together ... we laughed together ... we did almost everything together. My daughter would say on more than one occasion, *"When I grow up and marry, I want to be just like you!"* We were actually very happy. I just could not let go of Donnie.

Our pursuit, or should I say my obsession, to have children continued. As soon as we were settled, I got a job and hooked up with a new doctor. My medical records were transferred from my previous doctor and we discussed our next step which were fertility pills. I was told there was a good chance of multiple births, but I did not care. I wanted a baby and I wanted it no matter what I had to go through. My husband was working out of town now, so as long as I was happy, then he did not care how I proceeded. He only came home on weekends and he did not really have time to deal with all of this.

Time would pass, and nothing would be working out for me in the baby department. It was obvious by now that something was seriously wrong. You would think that looking on my medical records and seeing I had an abortion at such a young age would spark something, but it never did. Why? Because it was not something I shared openly. Yes, the doctor should have seen it when reading my medical history, but let's get real here for a minute, can we ... doctors do not read every single line of a medical chart. They peruse the chart and pick out what they see as relevant. I am sure by now the medical notes on my abortion were very well hidden in the depths of this chart. Unless I brought them to my new doctor's attention, they would not see them. I did not see me pointing this out!

Even today, when I am filling out medical forms, where it asks if you had any still births, etc., I will put no. I am so ashamed of what I did. It truly is a stigma which is difficult to overcome. My doctor never said anything because I did not bring it to her attention. If I was supposed to share this with her, then we were out of luck. Telling her would mean unlocking all of the junk on the inside of me which I had long ago buried. I was not ready to rehash my past. As time went by, however, I was getting desperate, so I was going to have to say something at some point.

Finally, I did share with my doctor what had happened. You have to realize that this was the hardest thing I had to do. I felt angry and ashamed all at the same time. It was not something I was proud of. Advising my doctor of this, of course, caused the course of action to change. It was time to run tests to see if I was even able to conceive.

By this time, both of my sisters had babies. My other sister getting pregnant was just as dramatic as it was with the first one. It drilled home even more to me how what happened to me had affected them. We were at my mother's house and I think we were having some sort of party ... Tupperware or something. My sister arrived and shortly thereafter she asked if she could speak to me in another room. I did not think anything about it at the time, but once again my failure to conceive would be right there ... *failure, failure, failure!* It was all I heard in my head. As we entered another room in my mom's house, my sister closed the door. When she turned around to look at me, she was already crying. I could not for the life of me imagine what was wrong. I asked her what was going on as I went to hug her, and she said, "*Please, do not hate me*". I could not even think of anything she could do that would make me hate her. My family was everything to me. I loved them more than humanly possible at times, so what in the world had made her think such a thing. The next words out of her mouth brought it all into focus … she was pregnant. I just stood there for what seemed like eternity, and then I realized I had to pull it together. I smiled, put my arms around her, and said, "*Sis, nothing could ever make me hate you. I am happy for you*". I must have been convincing because she believed me, and we returned to the living room where she shared her good news with everyone.

It amazes me sometimes how we can be in total turmoil on the inside and yet appear as though everything is fine on the outside. I must have smiled and appeared happy because no one said anything. I knew I was suffocating. I was angrier than ever, and I just wanted to get out of there. I felt as if the life was again being sucked out of me, and I thought I would quit breathing at any given moment. I played along, but I left as soon as the opportunity presented itself. I do not think the front door was fully shut before the tears and the anger welled up inside of me. Again, I hated my sister. I hated my parents. I hated Donnie. I hated everyone, and I was more convinced than ever that there was no such thing as a God. There could not be.

I dried my tears, and as always, I told myself I had to simply get over it. I put one foot in front of the other and I moved on. At some point, I would soon find out that even I had breaking points.

I could not bring myself to attend any baby showers. This was simply asking too much, and I refused to do it. I was so wrapped up in my pain that I could not see the pain I was causing my sisters. Too bad! They will have to deal with it, and I supposed they did.

My determination to have a child increased and it was all I ever thought about. The more I failed at this, the more I partied and drank. My husband and I were on softball teams, bowling teams, and we always surrounded ourselves with other partiers. We held huge parties every summer for the end of bowling … for the end of softball … any excuse to throw a party. We did it well. Some weekends when he would come home, he would just want to chill because he had been out of town all weekend. Now he was home and he wanted to enjoy being home. Not me ... I wanted to party!!!! I had been home all week and now I wanted to entertain.

My doctor had performed the first round of tests to see if I was the problem. She injected dye in my system which ran through my fallopian tubes to make sure they were open. I can remember the day we did this as if it were recently. I was sitting on the side of the bed as she explained to me what would happen. I was fighting with everything inside of me not to breakdown and cry. I was scared to death. I thanked God … *the God I was not sure even existed … the God I hated …* for the doctor I had. I said thank you to a God I assumed was listening. I had no real belief or even knew what that meant. It was not something I talked about. I did not allow conversations about God in my home. As far as I was concerned, it was all malarkey and I did not mind telling you the same should you ask.

The results of these tests were very critical. My fallopian tubes had to be open. What type of God would allow them to be closed? Not any God I desired to serve! *(Note: Many years later when I would give my heart and life to Christ, I came across a totally different struggle. One day I read Psalm 127:3, "Behold, children are a heritage from the Lord, the fruit of the womb a reward." Automatically I read this to mean that I was not good enough to have a child. God did not think me worthy; thus, He did not allow me to have children. I was devastated. Living in continual sin and away from God, I could not have children. Living in faith with God, He confirms my unworthiness. Oh my gosh, what do I do with this? It would take a lot of years to work this train of thought out of me, but God did! It was not a simple battle.)*

My doctor was compassionate and would be with me through many years. At times, she was my only source of relief. I could cry with her, but I would not cry with my husband or my family. Unless I was drunk, of course, then I would cry about it all the time. Sober I would not give anyone the satisfaction of seeing me breakdown.

A moment of reflection … as much as I have grown in my relationship with Christ over the years and have put this all behind me, I still fight with that part of me that will not break down in front of people. I want to cry sometimes in church during praise and worship … the presence of the Holy Spirit will be so great, and I can feel release coming, and then nothing. I have not been able to overcome completely, and I know it has caused hindrances with my relationship with Christ. He has so much more for me in life, but I need to give it all to Him. I am better at releasing my pain and emotions than I used to be during these years of my life, but I still struggle with this. I guess some things are more difficult to overcome than others. I pray about complete surrender and I ask that you pray for me also.

The test results came back a few days later. It was officially confirmed. I was the problem. One of my fallopian tubes was blocked. As a result, it had decreased my chances of conception by fifty percent. My doctor blamed this on my previous abortion. *(Note: I have tried to research all of this to see how it all comes into play medically but unfortunately my medical records did not share what I was seeking. For the most part, I could not get records. I am not sure how all of this comes into play, but I just know I was being punished for what I did. Whether my abortion was directly or indirectly responsible, I cannot say for sure. In my mind, however, it was all a direct result of my past sins.)*

I told my family about the blockage, but I did not share with them what I felt caused it. As much as I would have loved to use this to hurt those who shared in my abortion, I could not bring myself to hurt them anymore. I guess I was not as hard and inconsiderate as I thought I was. I still went on the premise that I had to protect my parents and not make them feel badly. As much as the anger at them was seething on the inside of me, I loved them so much and I would not bring more suffering to them. They tried so hard to be supportive and offer me love, but what they perceived as love and support, I interpreted as pity. It only fueled the anger inside of me. I did not need their pity and I did not want it.

Pity is another issue I continue to struggle with today, though not as badly as before. I have lost so many blessings

God has brought to me because I refuse to accept 'pity' from anyone. My interpretation of pity has hampered me from receiving. I am still a work in progress.

Caring people offer love and support. They are not offering pity. Not only did I lose out because of this incorrect mindset, but I also deprived many of receiving blessings for their act of reaching out.

Surgery was scheduled as I had decided to have reconstructive surgery to repair the tube. My doctor explained to me this was not a guarantee I would conceive. Even if I did get pregnant, the odds would be that I could only have one child and I would have to conceive rather quickly. Not only would the fallopian tube close right back up after conception, but there was also a good chance it would close again shortly after surgery. I did not care about odds. In my mind and for my own peace, I had to have this surgery. It was my one shot and I had to take it. It had to be successful. I felt as if my whole life was riding on this.

I had the surgery and I returned home to play the waiting game. Not long afterward I thought there must be a God in heaven because not only was the surgery successful, but I got pregnant immediately. I cannot put into words the joy I felt. At long last I can forgive myself and move on. I can forgive all the people I have harbored resentment towards. My parents can forgive themselves, and my siblings can let go of the fear I will hate them for having children. Finally, it is all going to work. I AM PREGNANT!!! I am going to have a baby and the world is good again.

I spent the next few days in a dream. I was planning the nursery in my head. I was looking at baby clothes and thinking of color schemes. I could physically feel the warmth of my child growing inside of me. It was all I ever wanted in life and it was finally becoming a reality. Nothing or no one could have brought me down from the top of the mountain. My daughter would finally have a sibling. I would have two wonderful children and my life would be complete. I did not care if my husband worked out of town and was hardly ever home. I was going to quit my job and be a full-time mother. I would bake cookies. I would be a soccer mom. I had it all figured out. Never mind I never did these things for my daughter … I would do them now. The pain and suffering I had felt in the past was worth this one moment of happiness. Nothing could have dampened my world at this time. I felt like I smiled all the time, even in my sleep. I probably looked like I was walking around with a hanger in my mouth because I was all smiles. I just wanted to scream to the world. I was going to be the best mom ever.

Chapter Fifteen

It never ceases to amaze me how you can go from being on the mountaintop and then fall into the pit in the matter of seconds. With life there are no guarantees. Happiness at times can seem like such an illusion and maintaining a sense of harmony is all too often short lived. It is why we should value every second of every day. All too often we are robbed of what we feel we deserve and come up empty handed. As with everything else up to this point, my joy would not last for long.

Let us be realistic here. I was already a mother, yet I was not baking cookies or doing all the things I proclaimed I would do now. *Why do you think this is?* It is because my anger in life was not just based solely on my inability to have children. Up to this point in my life, there were many reasons for my hidden anger. No amount of babies would change this until I sought help and dealt with why the anger was there in the first place … anger caused over the years by many things. Not having a child was only a portion of that anger. Granted it was probably the biggest portion, but it was not all of it. This is why alcoholics fail in life … why people can never truly turn their lives around. They think they can get a 12-step program and be fixed but it is only a temporary fix. You cannot get out of prison harboring years of hate, resentment, anger, and the like and just start a new life. You need to unload your past luggage first before you can be completely satisfied with your new luggage. Fixing the problems that arose out of the anger is great, but it does not fix what caused the anger, and it does not last forever. You need to fix what causes you to drink … do drugs … turn to this or that, before you can be healthy. I could have had twins, triplets, whatever, and it would not have mattered. I would still not have baked cookies anymore for this new child than I did for my daughter. I would have still been broken on the inside.

One night, early in my pregnancy, I awoke because I was having cramps in my stomach. I was only eight weeks pregnant and I was scared to death. I got out of bed and went into the bathroom and found blood. I immediately woke my husband and we went to the emergency room. It was the longest ride of my life. The hospital was about thirty minutes from where we lived, and I could not get there fast enough. I was crying silently because I was terrified if I broke down as I wanted to, I would cry the baby right out of me. *How silly was that?* I did not want to even breathe any more than I had to for fear it would cause a miscarriage. I was determined to hold on to this child. I found myself praying to a God I had doubted up until this point, and in no uncertain terms I told Him I could not lose this baby. I begged. I prayed.

Finally, we got to the hospital and I was told everything was fine, but I would have to be very limited in my activities. No heavy lifting. No long distant traveling. And absolutely no drinking. I did not care. I would do whatever it took to hold on to this child. *Please, God, just do not take this child from me.*

The God I did not believe in … the God I had no true perception of … the God I took for granted daily … He must have heard my pleas and I was once again on the mountaintop. How quickly my emotions went from one level to another. I was breathing normal again. I was glad I did not break down crying on the way to the hospital, because I was only overreacting. Everything was fine, and life was as it should be.

A few days later, we were invited to my sister-in-law's for a family get-together. She lived about an hour or so from our house. I knew my husband wanted to go and be with his family, but I was afraid of traveling that far from home. I knew I would not be able to drink. I started to feel a bit guilty though because I should not expect my husband not to drink. After all, he was not pregnant. I called my doctor and asked her could I make the trip. She said she felt it would be fine, but she advised me that if at any time I felt any discomfort, no matter how trivial, I was to return immediately. You would have thought her concern would have been enough to sway me from going but it did not. I had to go. It meant a lot to my in-law's and my husband said he thought everything would work out. I think he was getting a bit irritated with all my stressing over this pregnancy.

We went, and we had a nice time. He got to see his family, and I was glad I had come. I would have felt badly if I had of been the reason he missed being there. We spent the night and we would leave later the next day for home. When I got up the next morning, I felt uneasy for some reason. It was like I had this impending gloom hanging over my head or something. You know that feeling you get in the pit of your stomach from fear? I had it! I went into the bathroom, but everything appeared to be alright. I passed it off as my worrying too much. I could not eat breakfast though and I was not sure if it was because of morning sickness or my fears.

The day progressed, but I was very careful not to do anything more than I had to. I do not think I even got out of my chair much throughout the day. I was starting to have a discomfort I cannot really describe. I kept delaying telling anyone because I did not want to ruin the day for them. Finally, I could not take it any longer. I was worrying myself sick and I knew now it was not my imagination. Something was not right. I shared the thought with my husband that I felt we needed to return home, but he also thought I was worrying too much. A few hours later, I spotted blood and we left immediately for the hospital. Hours later it was over, and I was no longer pregnant.

The first emotion I felt was failure. It was as if every failure in my life up to this point was dangling over my bed as a reminder to me I was a total failure in all I set out to do. I told my husband I was sorry for failing him, but as always, he had a nonchalant attitude about it and reassured me it was no big deal. It was, however, a big deal to me. I felt as if I had buried someone very dear to me. Not only had I buried them, but I could not figure out why I was so distraught because I had never met them. However, I did know I had lost a daughter. Do not ask me how I knew because I cannot explain it, but I just knew. I gave her the name of Sarah Renee. Even though we had never met, I knew her. I pictured what she would look like. In my mind, I saw her start school … being a cheerleader in high school … graduation … leaving for college, and yes, I even saw her getting married. I ran her whole life through my mind in a very short time. How did one do things like that? I do not know. I just know I did.

I was simply numb. I just wanted to go home and become a recluse. I could not handle life if this was all I ever had to look forward to … one disappointment after another. Was I such a horrible person that God would not allow me to have a child? This is how my thought processes were going. I did not get much reassurance on the home front.

I do not think my husband was ever comfortable with emotions. His family was not as affectionate as most though they loved each other dearly. At times, he did not know how to handle my family who were very affectionate. I think he meant well, but he was not the comfort I needed. He never spoke much on the way home, and it was just as well. I did not have much to say. I could feel resentment and anger welling up inside of me at him and everyone. *Did he not realize all the implications of this? Did he not remember the doctor said my tube would close back up after this pregnancy? Did he not grasp how much this had meant to me?* I guess not. Why would it? He already had a son. I was the only one without a child. It seemed everyone else in my life had children, and then there was me … poor pitiful me! Never mind I had a beautiful daughter at home. Instead of looking at my many blessings in life, I **chose** to look at everything except my blessings. It is how I felt. I did, however, know one thing for certain. Under no circumstances did I want anyone to feel sorry for me. I did not need people's pity or sympathy, and I refused to accept it.

When we arrived home, I simply went to bed. I did not call my family immediately. I did not want to speak with anyone. Telling people I had lost the baby was the same to me as admitting to them I was again a failure. Just another failure in a long list up to this point. *Why did God even create me? What was the purpose of my life other than to take up space and be a punching bag for pain?*

I was back to square one. If possible, I was filled with even more contempt and anger. I returned to work and life went on.

Shortly after returning to work, I again went to see my OB/GYN. She was so compassionate with me. I felt as if she was the only person who truly understood. She advised me my options had not expired and I could choose to again have the reconstructive surgery. I left her office feeling as if the weight of the world was on my shoulders. *Could I possibly go through this yet again?* I knew how quickly my tube could close back up after surgery. What if I did not get pregnant right away and I had the surgery for nothing? Was it worth putting myself through a major surgery and 6 weeks of recuperation for something that was not guaranteed? Was I up to another miscarriage mentally? I was an emotional wreck and I simply did not know which way to turn.

Life has a way of giving you answers before you even contemplate the questions. It certainly did for me. One day as I was pondering my next course of action, and whether anything was worth another surgery, I started having lower abdominal pain. At first, I thought it was cramping, but it intensified to the point where I could not function in my daily routines. As hours passed, I ended up on the sofa hurting and running a fever. After twenty-four hours or so of this, I finally relented and went to the hospital.

By the time I reached the emergency room, my fever was high, and I was in a great deal of pain. The doctor decided I needed to go into surgery immediately as I had appendicitis and he was afraid it was about to rupture. I literally called my mom as they were prepping me. I was alone at the hospital.

I am not sure how long I was in surgery or how long I slept afterwards, but when I awoke I felt as if I had been through the wringer and back. I never knew anyone who had an appendectomy, but by the condition of my body, it was more complicated than I had anticipated. I was still in a lot of pain and felt as if I had been cut from side to side. I could not move much, and I was very sore and tender across my lower stomach. I would soon find out I had undergone major surgery for more than an appendectomy.

As the doctors explained it to me, when they cut me open to take out my appendix, they saw it was in good shape. Upon further investigation, they realized it was my tube that was about to burst. It was badly infected and there was not much they could do short of removing it. I was devastated. *How could this be? Why was this happening to me?* Again, I questioned whether I was such a bad person God could not see fit to give me some reprieve from this suffering? *Was I such a horrible mother to my daughter He could not allow me another child? Was I being punished?* I must have cried for what seemed like eternity until I finally dozed off. When I woke up, I knew one thing for certain … it was time to get off this emotional roller coaster and move on. I did just that!

I did move on but unfortunately, I moved in the wrong direction. I threw myself even more into the party world. I drank twice as much, and now my quest in life was to throw parties and be the best hostess! As I said, we had a pig roast for the end of softball season, the end of bowling season, the end of any season. We threw the biggest parties around, and they would last for weekends. All you had to do was show up. We had all the food, all the alcohol, live bands, and everything you could possibly want. Just come and have a good time. Party all weekend and say good-bye to my husband on Mondays. I was living the perfect life … care-free and fun! What more could I have asked for?

Since I had so much time on my hands during the week, I expanded my horizons and I made new friends. You would think being a full-time mother would have kept me busy.

My marriage was a farce on the inside, but on the outside, we had loads of friends. To the world around us, we were the ideal couple. We did everything together. Where you saw one, you saw both of us. We knew how to laugh and enjoy life.

I was still raising my daughter, but not the way I should have. I was there for her when she was going through difficult periods in her life but that was about the bulk of it. She had the best clothes. She had the prettiest bedroom. I made sure she was protected during our parties, but I was not a mom. When I should have been home helping her with homework, baking cookies, and just being her mom, I was too busy partying and entertaining. I was filling this emptiness inside of me with all the wrong things. I continued to bury all the pain I hid so well from the world even deeper.

Then, as life would have it, irony appeared yet again ... Donnie was home. On this day, I was working for a real estate agent in Charlottesville. He was a very handsome man and we did a lot of flirting during work hours. My mom predicted I would have an affair with this man, but I never did. As I sat at my desk, the telephone rang. It was Donnie on the other end. It had been years since I had seen or spoken to him. All those feelings resurfaced as if it were yesterday. I loved him just as much as I ever did, and I could not wait to see him. He was still married, but he was back in the states now and he wanted to see me. For once something seemed to be going my way. I was scheduled to show a house out in the country for my boss later that day, so Donnie and I planned on meeting there. I was as nervous as a young bride, and again I saw absolutely nothing wrong with what I was doing. Donnie and I were connected in ways people would never understand, and we deserved to see each other. Though we were married to other people, in our hearts I wanted to believe we saw it differently.

It was not our fault we were not together. It was his parents' fault … it was my parents' fault … it was God's fault! Anyone I could come up with to blame for our not being together, I did. Of course, the blame game also helped me justify what I was doing. The fact this would hurt my husband and daughter if they ever found out, or that it would hurt Donnie's wife and children never occurred to me. Obviously, it did not occur to Donnie either. Even if it did, I did not care. I had suffered enough, and I deserved to see him. *Entitlement … we always feel as if we are entitled to what we want and do not have.* In the real world, we are not entitled to anything. It is only through God's grace and mercy we deserve what we have in life. He paid the ultimate price for us, yet we fool ourselves into thinking it is we that deserve this and that. It is amazing how we can reason things out in our mind to the point where we feel justified in what we do. I think I lived most of my life doing just that.

Donnie and I met as we had planned, and we spent a few hours together. It would prove to be a difficult time for both of us. For once I lost it with him and shared some of my pain. I do not know how we even got to the point of talking about the past, but I could no longer hold my anger in. I told Donnie how I hated him for having children. How I hated him for what he had done to me. How I hated him for costing me the formidable price of never being able to have children. He was shocked, and we cried together. We did not have enough time to really console one another. Irony would win again, and we parted ways. *Did bearing my soul to him help?* No. I think it made it worse. I thought if I bared my soul to him, then he would leave his wife, I would leave my husband, and we would live happily ever after. It did not happen that way and I left there angrier than when I went, if that was possible. All I could think about was the fact that Donnie was returning to his life with his children. I was returning to mine with none. Where was the justice in all of this? Again, was I such a horrible person that God could not see fit to allow me to have only one child? Donnie had several! My husband even had one! My sisters had babies. My friends had babies. Where was mine? All I wanted was one. Was this truly too much to ask?

I resumed life as it had been with all the drinking and partying. As my husband was still working out of town, I lived alone with my daughter, but she had her own life! She was grown now and had a driver's license. During the week it was just me and then my other half would return on weekends. Our relationship was deteriorating rapidly. I tried to tell him he needed to quit his job and come home. I knew I could not hold on much longer. I needed him at home with me every night. I needed to be a family as I thought a family should be. I wanted what I craved. Had he relented and come home, I am not sure it would have solved anything.

One Monday stands out in my mind more than any as it was truly the beginning of the end. As I walked my husband to the door on this morning, as I always did, I kissed him good-bye and said, "*You need to come home. We are losing this marriage*". As was the norm with him, he kind of chuckled and told me I worried too much. I just could not get it through his head we were treading on very thin ice.

Almost six years after we finally separated, I would learn the truth as to why my husband did not want to quit working out of town. He had girlfriends all over the place and even had a few affairs with friends of mine. It was told to me he had been unfaithful to me since the day we married. When I learned of this, however, I was at a good place in my life and I would not react as I would have done years earlier. If anything, I felt sorry for him. God was the center in my life now, and I had no reason for anger and bitterness anymore. How horrible it must have been for him to live life as he had. On top of that, I wondered to myself if he could have possibly brought a disease home which could have infected me and caused me to not be able to conceive. Of course, this was not true. My abortion was the direct cause of my inability to conceive, but I guess I wanted to blame him as much as possible. Ironically, however, I felt I was just getting what I deserved since I had seen Donnie numerous times during our marriage. I guess it was just another failure I would have to accept.

Many years later, while I was in town filling my car with gas, I heard someone call my name. When I turned my head towards the direction I thought I heard my name being called, I saw a girl crossing over the traffic circle, waving her hand in my direction. As she drew near to me, I realized it was a girl I had bowled with and been friends with for quite some time. As she got closer to me, I remembered she was one of the girls I had been told slept with my ex-husband. As all of this was coming to my mind, for a split second … just a flash of time, I could feel anger welling up on the inside of me. By the time she reached me and threw her arms around me, the Holy Spirit convicted me for my anger. At this point, I could smell alcohol on her breath and she looked like she was doped up. I simply held her in my arms and said a silent prayer for her. By the looks of things, her life had not changed much over the years. I, on the other hand, had so much to be thankful for. My relationship with Christ had separated me from that lifestyle and it was very apparent she needed my hug more than my condemnation. If Christ could forgive me for all I had done in life, then who was I not to forgive her? Amazing how far He had brought me and the healing He had given me from the inside out.

My husband and I would remain married for 15 years, and we would separate four months after our daughter left for college. My life was in worse shape now than ever before, and I had no idea who I was anymore. Again, I questioned my purpose in life. I had failed everyone who ever entered my life.

Because of the pent-up anger and bitterness on the inside of me, I managed to push people away. One such case has haunted me to this very day. For years, I had a very close friend. We were inseparable. We had so much fun together and she spent more time at my house than anywhere. She was like a sister to me and I loved her dearly. How do you mistreat people you love? Do you push them away because they have what you cannot have? Well, I did. One day she told me she was pregnant, and it ended our friendship. I do not exactly remember how it went down, but I know it was never the same between us. I lost her, and I lost being a part of this special time in her life. She had twins and I would not be there for her or them. We have since reconnected, but as much as I long for it to be as it was, too many years have passed. We are congenial to one another … we had lunch once, but it is no more than that. Too much time has passed and too much has happened in each of our lives for us to be able to just turn the clock back. I take full responsibility for the demise of our friendship, and it is just another failure I carry to this day.

Looking back over the years, I lost more than I ever gained except for my relationship with Christ. People who I thought were my true friends … people who I truly loved and cared for … simply discarded me when my marriage broke up. There was one couple who my ex-husband and I partied with all the time … we played cards together … we hung out … and I loved them so much. Then, one day, they … or should I say 'she' turned her back on me. I have never figured it out. I am certain it is because of lies she was told from another party I was acquainted with, but I guess I will never know. I have practically begged her to tell me, but to no avail. I guess she did not love me like I thought she did. I still miss her immensely. *How do people just cut you out of their lives*? I have never been able to do that. Yes, I pushed people away, but I never simply let them go because of what someone else said or did. I love people who enter my life with a passion, and it has caused me more pain than it should.

Chapter Sixteen

Where was my hope? Was drinking and partying all that was left? I could only assume it was because I did it even more. I spent the majority of my nights in bars, and I wrapped myself in false relationships that ended up going nowhere. I was basically estranged from my family. Sure, I showed up for family gatherings. I turned up when I found out a family member had a need. Otherwise, I kept my distance. They knew nothing about me or my life. I preferred it that way and so it began … a never-ending cycle with even more time spent alone and tons of confusion.

Even though my marriage was pretty much over and I was living with a friend, we tried to date periodically and put the marriage back together. During this time, I was also involved with another man. *Pretty messed up, huh?* I truly was very confused about life and what I wanted out of it.

I was currently working at a camp for children with handicaps. It was during this time that I met another guy who would fast become an extension of me. He and I bonded from the moment we met. He was the maintenance supervisor at the camp and I worked in the office. We had a lot in common. For years to come, he would be my safe haven. I never felt alone in life because he was only a phone call away. We partied together. He held me when I cried. He listened to me. He always had time for me. He was in a tumultous relationship with his girlfriend. Though they lived together, she was constantly moving in and out. On more than one occasion I would show up on his doorstep to pull him away for the evening. It was fine with his girlfriend because she knew our relationship was purely platonic. As years passed, I began to wonder why he and I did not see if we could have more than friendship. Over time, though we never acted on it, I would find out he felt the same. I guess we both feared losing one another so we chose to remain friends. Sadly, however, we did lose one another. He was here for a very special season in my life. I pray for him daily as it has been years since I last saw or spoke to him.

Eventually the house of cards my husband and I built came crashing down. He found out about the other man in my life. He gave me the house and moved elsewhere. Before leaving, however, he did me one last honor and he escorted me to a function for my job. When we returned to the house, things got sort of ugly between us and he left. I went out shortly thereafter and caught up with some friends. By the time I got home, I was plastered. I do not even remember how I got home. Though I had been drinking pretty much all evening, I knew I was not ready to call it a night. I sat on the sofa and began to simply cry. Look at the mess my life was in. I had pretty much destroyed any plans of a successful future in anything. I was separated from my husband, I had no contacts with Donnie, and I was involved with another man. *How much worse could I mess things up*?

After a few hours of sitting there, I started to think back over my life. In doing so, I could not think back without dredging up the abortion and what I had done to my unborn child. Then, to make matters even worse, I had to admit out loud that I felt responsible for the miscarriage I had suffered. You see I felt personally responsible for the loss of my unborn child ... *the daughter I never got to meet ... the daughter I killed.* Yes, I carried deep inside of me the guilt for yet another murder of an unborn child.

I never ever told anyone what I am about to share with you. The shame and guilt were too much for me to admit this to myself much less share it with another human being. It was during the writing of this book that God brought this to my remembrance. The rot and stench I carried deep on the inside of me had festered to the point where the odor was horrendous, and it was eating me alive.

Do you remember I shared earlier that my doctor said I could travel to my in-law's cookout, but I had restrictions to abide by? One of those restrictions was that I not drink alcohol. This was very difficult for a party girl like me and even more difficult for someone who felt they knew it all. I realize this all is in such conflict with the part of me which was so desirous to have a child. I understand how you must be thinking, *"Wow, I cannot believe she had alcohol. She deserved to lose that child!"* You are not saying anything to yourself that I have not said to myself a hundred times or more each day since I lost my daughter. The guilt was like a cancer on the inside of me, steadily eating away at any healing I sought however I sought it. I had one mixed drink on the day prior to my miscarriage. For years upon years, I would always feel that the one mixed drink I had was what destroyed my child. It was why God chose to render me childless, so that I would never be able to conceive a child of my own.

Now home alone and drunk ... sitting on my sofa ... I became so emotional and depressed I was screaming on the inside. When you are filled with so much anger, it eventually had to come out. I raised myself off the sofa and started breaking everything in the house I could get my hands on. I guess I thought I could expend my anger in this way. I am not sure how long this went on, but when the rampage was over, I knew I was in serious trouble emotionally and I needed help.

Being the person I was and raised to think weakness was an impurity in my life, I could not bring myself to reach out to anyone. I knew I was on the brink of doing something terrible, but yet I could not call out to people I knew loved me and cared for me. I so desperately wanted to reach out, but I simply could not. I am not sure how long I struggled with this emotional tug of war on the inside, but eventually I picked up the telephone attempting to get help. I had to … I was literally dying on the inside. Several times I called one of my sisters, but I would only let it ring a few times and hang up. If I remember correctly, it was every bit 2:00 or 3:00 in the morning. *How was I going to get help if I did not say anything*? I did not know but I kept on doing it.

My sister later told me that she had a caller identification box hooked up to her telephone. I never gave it much thought as I continually telephoned her over and over. At some point, I was incapable of thinking rationally at all. When my sister saw it was me calling and the hour of the morning, she began to worry. To make matters even worse, each time I would call her, she would answer but I would not respond when she picked up the telephone. After this had happened two or three times, she decided to call my other sister who lived a short distance from me. They agreed that something was amiss, and they needed to get to my house. She explained what had been transpiring up to that moment and that she was on her way. However, in the interim she needed my other sister to start in the direction of my house since she lived much closer to me and could get there more quickly.

When my sister arrived at my house, she had to push glass away from the door to enter. As I remember, I was simply sitting on the sofa crying. Shortly after she arrived, my other sister got there. I do not remember exactly the way it went down, but I think when they asked me if I was alright that I responded either "no" or "I don't know". They became very concerned. Obviously, I needed help, or I would not have contacted them to begin with. After some talking, one of my sisters finally called a local hospital to seek advice on what to do. I had, by this point, admitted I was in a bad way and I needed help to get back on my feet. During the conversation with the hospital, they asked my sister if I was a danger to myself. When she relayed this question to me, I do remember saying, "*I don't know. I simply do not know*". I did not know how to answer that question because I did not know what I was capable of.

I would like to think I would never have harmed myself. I truly feel I loved my parents too much to put them through something like that, and I know for a fact my mother could never have handled the loss of one of her children. They were her life. My parents were too old to have to deal with stuff like this, but my response to my sister just goes to show the state of mind I was in and the depth of depression I had sunk to. Then there was my daughter. Though I was not the mother I desired to be, I loved her dearly. How could I even contemplate putting her through such an ordeal? Had she not already been through so much?

The process in which I reached out for help also showed how difficult it was for me to be vulnerable. I simply did not have the capacity in me to be weak or admit I needed someone. I had been so hurt, mostly by my own choices in life, that I was rock solid, especially on the inside when it came to opening up or seeking counsel that I needed. Nevertheless, it did not stop me from abusing myself or allowing people to use me and treat me unfairly. It was as if I were two separate individuals housed in the same body.

I would be admitted to a hospital for a week and go into serious counseling. During this time, I refused to see anyone. I just wanted to be left alone. The medical staff would not leave me alone and I had to meet certain criteria before I could be released. Knowing this, I did what I had to … I said what was expected so I could go home. I do remember at one point that they called my husband in for a counseling session with me. He was still very angry and hurt over the demise of our marriage, and though we were not divorced, I think he felt personally responsible for me. On the other hand, he used the first opportunity he could to hurt me. He told me as he was leaving the hospital that I had not done anything he had not already done. At this point, you need to remember that I knew of no infidelity in our marriage except for my own. As far as I was concerned, he was the perfect husband and I had failed him as I had everyone else in my life. He used this to his advantage.

You can pretty much assume by now that I felt as low as any individual could go. I felt as if I were walking around with a big red "X" marked on me to show I was a wife who was unfaithful. I would carry that mentality around for a very long time, until I allowed Christ to remove it. As I am typing this today, I can tell you without any doubt whatsoever that if Christ had not entered my life, I would still be hauling that "X" around. I was incapable of forgiving myself. Even when I finally let Christ into my life, it would take years of loving me, forgiving me, and being very easy with me before Christ could get me to forgive myself.

Returning home from the hospital, I had no hope, no plans, and just a day-to-day existence. Of course, the world did not see this person because on the outside I was always laughing and being the person I was supposed to be. *Who was that person*? I did not even know anymore. I drifted from job to job, and nothing in life seemed to fill this crater in the pit of my gut.

I did have one saving grace during this time in my life and she was my best of friends. She would become the best friend I ever had or would ever have again. She and I had met shortly after I relocated to Gordonsville. We were so connected in everything. We thought alike. We both partied like fools, and we were always there for one another. She truly was a part of me. I have often heard it said how people search their whole lives for the 'soul mate' God has for them. Well, if there could be a 'soul mate' in friendships, then she was mine. We fought together. We cried together. We drank together. We did it all. She was such a vital part of my life, and then I would lose her too. One Thanksgiving Day she passed out and that would be the end. Nobody will ever know the loss I felt. I went through the motions, handled the funeral on my own, but I think my heart was getting harder by the minute. I can remember sitting at her funeral all alone. No one in my family was available to go with me. I remember thinking to myself about the person seated next to me, "*Please, just reach over and touch me. Put your hand on my hand or something. I need to feel that someone cares*". I was crying so badly, and I just needed to feel physical touch and know I was not alone. Of course, the person beside me had no inkling of what I was thinking. From the outward appearance I was conveying to all those around me, I am sure they thought I was handling things just fine. Little did I know, however, that I was not alone!

Even if I did not always give credit where credit is due, I had one thing in my corner through all of this. By this time in my life, I was truly walking with the Lord. I was a new Christian and believer in Christ and it was more than enough to carry me through. I could feel the presence of His Spirit right there beside me and it gave me enough comfort to sustain. I had not been a Christian long and I did not know a lot about walking with Him. It was still all a learning process. However, during this very difficult time, He was right there with me. He has been carrying me ever since and I would not give up my relationship with Him for anyone or anything. He has turned me around and put me back on solid ground.

Chapter Seventeen

They say time heals all, but I know that is not always the case. Years would pass before I would learn from my sisters of my mom's guilt about the abortion. My mom had shared with them how she was the reason for everything I had gone through. She too had been suffering on the inside, being eaten away with guilt at the decision she and my dad made for me. When I heard this, I cried on the inside because we did not have the capabilities to share our pain. By the time of my mother's death in September of 2004, we had never spoken about the abortion or anything for that matter. It was not to be, and it is probably the biggest regret of my life. I loved my mom so much, and I would have given anything if we could have found cleansing in the arms of each other. We could not though, and now she is gone. Again, as with abortion, it is final and not something I can redo.

In 1997, prior to walking with Christ and after many years of dealing with the fact I could not have children, it would come to a conclusion once and for all. Over the course of time, I had many female problems and even had signs of early cancer in the uterus. My doctor thought it best I have a complete hysterectomy. Though in my mind I knew I could not conceive, I think a small part of me held on daily to the hope that I would. Now they wanted to take that little bit of hope I had been holding onto. It truly was the straw that broke the camel's back. I did not think I could take much more. I could not fight this any longer. It had been a lifetime battle and I was ready to concede defeat once and for all. I was physically, emotionally, and mentally worn out. I had to let it go and I did. It was truly a devastating time in my life.

I had the hysterectomy in February of 1997. How ironic that it was Valentine's Day. A day where others were receiving love through flowers, candy, and jewelry, I was conceding defeat and letting go. No sense in even thinking about it anymore. God had blessed many people that I knew of who had abortions with children, but it was not to be the case for me. I was not a Christian at this point in life. If there was ever a slim chance I would walk with the Lord one day, it was gone now. I did not want to even discuss religion and I wanted no part in going to church. *What had He ever done for me but cause me heartache? Why would I even want to think about serving a God like that?*

You need to understand that I was not brought up in a Christian home. The only time I heard God's name was during times of trial, and believe me, there were plenty of them in our family. However, as much as I heard my mother pray to God or cry out to God during difficult times, I could not for the life of me figure out what good it did. Nothing ever seemed to turn out well. *What was the use*? This was the mentality I had when it came to faith in God, but little did I know my life was about to take such a drastic turn for the better and all praise and glory to Him.

You wake up in the morning ... the sun is shining ... and for all appearances it is just another day. Then, in the blink of an eye, it becomes an historical day in your life.

By this time, my daughter had a child and was married. Our relationship was not bad, but it was not as it should have been. She was a good daughter in that I never had much trouble with her. She was a good student in school and never brought me much heartache. Nowhere near the heartache I brought to my mom. I was proud of the life she had built for herself and I missed her. My baby was grown and gone.

I was alone, dating yet another man, when I received a call that would alter the course of my life permanently. Someone I knew was in a bad way. To add insult to injury, she discovered she was pregnant. For the sake of privacy, I will refer to this individual as Sylvia.

Sylvia and I were very close. We had been in each other's lives for years. She was living out-of-state as her husband was in the military. After the birth of her second child, she soon realized she was pregnant again. Her marriage, as I would later learn, was a mess. There was a lot of abuse (physically, mentally, and emotionally). It was not a good situation at all, and I suspect her husband was also having an affair.

When Sylvia discovered she was pregnant, it did not bring with it the joy a pending pregnancy should bring. There were no reasons for celebration. She was living in hell here on earth, and she was terrified about what to do. She had two small sons, one still in diapers. I would not learn of her pregnancy for a few months, or of the conditions she and her sons were living in. However, out of desperation and not knowing what to do, Sylvia would finally tell me the truth about her marriage.

By this time, I was divorced and for a little over a year I had been dating someone. It was not a good relationship any more than the others I had been in since my divorce. *How could it be*? I was even more scarred by my past than ever, and I was lugging around with me all the past pains, disappointments, anger, and hostility. I was drinking like a fish and staying in bars a great deal of the time. I do not know how I managed to work considering I stayed out almost every night until 2:00 or 3:00 in the morning, but I did. I would, however, go through many jobs.

Though my boyfriend and I cared about each other a great deal, I think my neediness, my insecurities, and all the scars I was harboring on the inside of me were proving to be detrimental to us. Of course, if you were to ask me, I was fine, and life was good. Besides my problems, my boyfriend had issues of his own. We were not a match made in heaven by a long shot. I was drinking and partying as much as ever. As with most of the men I dated, I met my boyfriend in a bar. Though I had known of him for many years, I did not know him personally or think anything about him. I would see him a lot when I played pool as he was a very skilled pool player. After we got together, he would share with me how he had waited over three years to date me. Every time he thought it was a good time to ask me out on a date, I was already dating someone else. *Isn't that typical of a person with all the hidden secrets I had*? We never leave one relationship until we know there is another in the wings. I truly wore my insecurities on my sleeve, but if anyone else ever saw them, they did not bother to share it with me.

My boyfriend was not a heavy drinker even though he was in bars quite a bit. He knew I was. Once we made our relationship exclusive, he tried to get me to give up my drinking and partying ways. I remember asking him once why he ever wanted to date me if drinking was such an issue for him. He advised me he knew if he could just get to date me, then he could change me over time. Not a good way to begin a relationship. But isn't that what we think a lot of the times in our lives … that we can change the person we love. This concept probably has destroyed many good relationships. We are incapable of changing ourselves, much less changing other people. We do not realize this until we come to the knowing grace of Jesus. He is the only one that can change us, and He does so from the inside out. Try telling this to someone like me though! I wanted no part of Jesus, God, religion, or anything remotely connected. It was too late for me to be saved by anyone.

My boyfriend was a good man and a hard worker. He did not want to give up on me, but eventually he had no choice. I was not going to change.

When I learned of Sylvia's situation, I did not know what to advise her. I could not tell her to have an abortion, but I saw no easy fix to this dilemma. She was literally fighting for her life, and she could not even grasp the concept of bringing another child into this relationship. She had contemplated having an abortion, but the thought physically made her ill. It was murder in her eyes and nothing more. *What could I say*? Abortion had already ruined my life.

Sylvia knew of my abortion, but it was not because I shared it with her. Someone else took that liberty. *Can you imagine that?* On the day I was told that Sylvia knew of my abortion, I was furious. I jumped in my car and went to confront the individual I had trusted with this part of my life. I could not for the life of me understand why she felt the need to share this with Sylvia. She tried to give me an explanation, but I was having none of it. I knew secrets about her I could have shared with others, especially her two daughters, and I said as much to her. However, I was not raised that way. I would never have used the things I knew to get even with her. It simply is not what a friend does.

Sylvia and I discussed other options for her, especially adoption. She struggled with the thought of having strangers raise her child. After many conversations, she finally realized this was the only option she had. As for what her husband felt about the situation, I did not know, nor did we ever discuss it. I think this marriage was pretty much over as it was, and Sylvia was simply trying to do what was best for her other two sons and the unborn child she was carrying.

I was working a temporary position in Richmond at the time, and I had met Susan. She was a wonderful young lady and I really liked her and her husband. We became fast friends. One day she had confided in me and shared the fact she and her husband were having problems conceiving. When Sylvia finally relented to the idea of adopting her unborn child out, I immediately thought of Susan. I told Sylvia what I knew of the situation, and then I went to work and spoke with Susan. It seemed like it was a perfect match for all involved, plus Sylvia would be able to know where the child was. I gave Sylvia Susan's telephone number and they connected. I thought it was a done deal and they could just work out the particulars for themselves. I stepped out of the equation.

A few weeks after I had introduced Susan and Sylvia to one another, Sylvia called me to let me know the adoption idea with Susan was not going to work. From what I gathered from Susan later, she was not comfortable with the level of contact Sylvia wanted to have in the child's life. Though Sylvia was giving her unborn child up for adoption, she could not bring herself to cutting the child out of her life entirely. It was a very delicate situation.

During all of this, I was still dating my boyfriend. Reverting back to my sense of responsibility for the people in my life, I discussed with him how he would feel about us adopting the baby. The more I talked about it, the more excited I got. *Could this possibly work? How in the world would my boyfriend and I parent a child together when we cannot even go more than a month or so without splitting up? Was I delusional?* Well, lo and behold, he agreed. *Can you believe that?* One thing for certain, I was not going to give him much chance to think it over for fear that once he truly weighed the pros and cons of the situation, he would realize it was a crazy idea. I was almost 42 years of age, and he was 48. *How was this going to work?*

I had to think about how to broach this subject with Sylvia. I knew I would have to handle it very carefully, and I did. After we both thought about it, we decided it was the only way to go. Sylvia could still be a part of the child's life, and me … well, it would be nothing short of a dream come true. Now I just had to figure out a way to contain my excitement in the meantime. Plus, every morning I lived with the fear Sylvia would change her mind.

I shared this situation with my family, and though they were very, very concerned for Sylvia and what this would do to her, you could see how excited they were for me. It was truly a difficult situation. I am sure my family was torn between their happiness for me and their sense of concern for Sylvia. They knew how much Sylvia meant to me and she was a huge part of my family. All I could see was I was going to be a real mom … I was going to have that tiny person look to me for everything … I would see its little arms reach up for me and hear it call me mommy. As happy as I was, it was also a very terrifying time for me. It did nothing to improve my already insecure mind.

During the latter part of Sylvia's pregnancy, she had a lot of health issues. I was living with my boyfriend by this time because I had lost my home to a fire in February of that year (1998). How we managed to be in the same house for longer than a week is beyond me. Here I was basically homeless, jobless, and living with a man where there was constant turmoil, and yet I was thinking of becoming a mother at my age. I am sure some people thought I was delusional. However, my best friend was not one of those people. She was crazy about the idea, and we would joke around and tell people we were having a baby. This child would be as much a part of her life as it would be mine.

I had settled with the insurance company for the fire, so I had a little bit of money in the bank. I decided to fly to California and be with Sylvia during the final days of her pregnancy. I hated to do this because of how I felt about her husband, but she needed me more. While I was gone, my boyfriend would set up the crib and get things ready for us to return. What a happy family I convinced myself we would be. Who knows, maybe having a baby between us will improve our relationship. *Can you believe I had thoughts like this?* It was as if I thought this baby would make my world all better. As much happiness as this baby would bring to me, I still had a load of issues. Having babies would not make my life right. However, isn't this what people think at times? How many people thought they could improve their marriages by having a baby? How many women have had babies as a means of holding on to hold their man? How many young girls have gotten pregnant on purpose to hold on to their boyfriends? A baby was not a solution. I needed help in ways I never even thought. How unfair to bring a baby into a situation that is only going to get worse with an added dimension to it.

I truly saw the dire straits of Sylvia's marriage when I arrived at her home. Sylvia literally had no food in the house. When I say no food, I mean not so much as a cracker. How she had survived up to this point was beyond me. Her husband was spending most of his time away from home, and I guess his paychecks went with him. I was so heartbroken to think she had been living like this. I immediately took her and her two sons to Costco and bought groceries. I remember I spent over $400 that day. I was just so happy to be able to provide for them. You could tell how uncomfortable Sylvia was about this situation. I guess in her mind she was embarrassed even though she had no cause to be. This fiasco was not her doing. The only thing I can fault her for is using poor judgment in the man she married, but I guess, as with many things in life, we never see the true person we are involved with until it is too late. I know I had made way too many mistakes to be pointing fingers now.

While I was staying with Sylvia, I had contact with my ex-husband. Up until this point, we had remained friends even though he was in Maryland living with another woman. When he found out what I was contemplating, he became angry. I am not sure why, but it would put a permanent wedge between us. As of today, I have not spoken to him since. It is sad because I miss our friendship. I can only speculate that he was angry over the fact that while we were married we never could have a child and now I was having one.

Chapter Eighteen

June 19, 1998, Sylvia gave birth to a son. I named him Christopher William Molton. My boyfriend and I had picked out the name before I left. By this time, I had returned to using my maiden name which was Molton. As excited as I was over all of this, I tried to keep it in perspective for Sylvia's sake. I wanted her to know she could change her mind if she had to. I did not want her to do anything or make this final until she had a chance to truly grasp the reality of it all. I knew once I boarded that plane for Virginia with my son, there would be no turning back. I would fight to the bitter end to hold on to him. Because of this, I had to make Sylvia hold the baby and be as much a part of this as she would allow. Sylvia had scars of her own from an unstable life and this was not helping her at all.

As I held my son for the first time, I just wanted to drop to my knees and cry. I had an overwhelming sense of joy I never knew. This was the day I had longed for all of my life. I had a son … someone who was untouched by the cruelties of life … someone who would love me unconditionally … someone who would need me … someone who did not care about my past! My moment had arrived, but I still had to conceal all of this. I had to think of Sylvia and just play according to her reactions and emotions. It was a balancing act for me, but hadn't my whole life been a balancing act up to this point. Always feeling one thing on the inside and conveying another on the outside. I was a pro! I must have reserved some sense of decency through everything for me to be so concerned for Sylvia. Maybe I was not as hard as I felt!

The following day we left the hospital, but I could not return to Sylvia's home with Christopher. I did not want to be around her husband any longer. Previously I had to be around him for the sake of Sylvia and her sons, but now was a different story. I did not want her husband anywhere near Christopher.

Sylvia and I arranged to spend my final night at a hotel. This would allow us to have some private time together. I booked a room not far from the airport. Sylvia, her two sons, Christopher and I had a wonderful evening together. It allowed the boys to play with their new infant brother and it gave Sylvia some additional time to try to come to grips with the situation. It would prove harder on her than she had anticipated. During her pregnancy, Sylvia did everything not to get attached to this child. In her mind, she was successful. Now, however, she would see it was impossible. I think the only thing that got her through this was the fact that I was the one taking her son and the fact that she had two other sons she had to worry about. She truly felt in the depths of her heart she was doing what was best for everyone. Her emotional and mental pain put aside, she put the welfare and needs of everyone else first. I admired her for doing this.

Sylvia not only gave me the best gift any person ever could, but she truly did what was in the best interest of all parties regardless of her own suffering. It was truly a selfless act. Many children would be better off today if their biological mothers had given them up to a good loving home instead of keeping them in a bad situation.

This reminds me of the story of Moses in the Bible. His birth mother had to save him from the King who had ordered all firstborn sons to be murdered. In the end she saved his life, but she had to watch another woman raise him. Daily she was eye witness to her son being loved and cuddled by a woman who was an enemy to her and her family. From afar, she silently loved this child. The pain she carried ... the loss she felt ... the void in her heart ... she put all of this aside because she placed the welfare of her child above her own.

Sylvia sacrificed her emotional needs and put her love of her son first. She allowed him to be adopted when in her heart she loved him so much. She was a part of his life from a distance. Can you imagine how difficult this had to be? You see your child … the one you gave birth to … but he calls another woman 'mom'. People, please, do not make light of this. It had to be the purest form of love … to put the welfare of another above your own. To carry a child inside of you for nine months, then pass him to another. I am not sure I could be so selfless. This is exactly what Sylvia did!

Our departure at the airport was very emotional as you can well imagine. I would later learn Sylvia finally had to seek counseling to get through this. It was a time in her life where she suffered more than anyone could even imagine. Today Sylvia is a very healthy young lady and remarried to a wonderful man. She is raising their awesome son and together they raised her other two sons. Her husband has treated her and her sons wonderfully. He has provided well for all of them, and I am thankful to God for him every day. We all have come through this much better people.

It was finally time for me to depart and be on my way. Our good-byes were very emotional all around, but we managed to get through it. When I arrived at Dulles Airport, my boyfriend was waiting for me. I was excited to introduce him to his son. He had one son from a previous marriage, but due to a lot of circumstances beyond his control, he was not an active participant in his son's life. Our son was named after him and his other son. Of course, Christopher would carry my legal name of Molton.

It was almost midnight before we arrived back at our home with Christopher. When we pulled into the driveway, there was my mother, bless her heart, and my two sisters. They had been waiting for hours for us to arrive. They had a cake and balloons, and they could not wait to meet the newest member of the family. I think my mother was happier than I had seen her in a very long time. Christopher's arrival seemed to smooth out and soften some of the hardness of life we had endured. I was finally holding in my arms a baby … an infant … someone who belonged to me and whom I would love no matter what. It would take me a very long time, if I ever have, to accept the fact that he was mine. I wanted nothing more than to prove I could be a good mother. Our first night home and we were all wide awake with excitement. As the evening wore on, I decided it was time to get my son down for the evening. I had yet to unpack. While away, I had purchased an extra suitcase just for Christopher's things. I had bought quite a bit while away. I reached for the suitcase. As I unzipped and lifted the top, you can well imagine my dismay to see a case full of books. What in the world had happened to my son's things? I now had to acknowledge that the only things my son had were literally the clothes on his back. No formula! No diapers! No nothing! I had mistakenly grabbed the wrong suitcase when leaving the airport.

Frantically I called the airport to discover that the individual who had my suitcase had returned it to the airport. We could come and pick it up. In the meantime, what was I going to do? My boyfriend went to one of the all-night grocers and got me a few things to tide me over. He then left for the airport to retrieve the correct suitcase and return the one I had. So much for proving my mothering skills!

Today my son is 19 years of age, and there are still times when I catch myself simply staring at him in amazement. I could not love him, or my daughter, any more than I do even though I did not give birth to them. They truly are my daughter and my son, and I am truly their mother.

My relationship with my boyfriend soon ended. This was no surprise. However, he has proven to be a devoted father to Christopher. For many years, we would co-parent Christopher actively and together without so much as a quarrel. We vacationed together, visited places together, and shared holidays together. It was our greatest desire to give Christopher as normal a home life as we could. We truly were better off apart than together. Though we have not been romantically involved since Christopher was only a few months old, we are, to this very day, raising an amazing son and doing it well.

It would not be until August of 1998 that I would have a home to bring Christopher to and call our own. When my boyfriend and I separated shortly after Christopher was born, I lived with my sister and her family. I could not have been happier as a mom and my best friend was right there with me. Her friendship, as it had been so much in the past, was truly a saving grace for me. I miss her so much today. I know she and Christopher would have been great together. He has a lot of interests she had, and they would have had fun together. I have kept her alive in his mind. He still has the gifts she gave him during his baby shower, and we speak of her often. We still see her family from time to time. Christopher knows her and what she meant to me.

Chapter Nineteen

Though I had the one thing I longed for in my life, nothing had changed really. I was still drinking and partying as much as ever. I used a babysitter when I went out and I was back to work full time. Once again, though I was only fooling myself, I thought life was good. I had conquered the biggest hardship in my life, but I had not dealt with all the junk I had been hauling around on the inside of me for most of my life. As happy as I was, I could not figure out why I felt this big void in my life. What could it be? What was it that had not been fulfilled? I could not seem to get things under control and be the mother I dreamed of being. I wanted to be that mother so desperately, but I was incapable of it. This concept only furthered my sense of insecurities and I was turning to alcohol and partying as a solution.

During this time, I was working for a construction site as an Office Manager. I loved it. I met some wonderful people on this job and I learned so much. My babysitter's husband worked on the construction site, and she would sometimes bring lunch to her husband. When she did, she would bring my precious son with her. It would always be the highlight of my day. The workers would take him out on the job site and it was so cute. One day when I came to work, one of the workers had purchased two white rabbits for Christopher and made a cage. I was so excited to take them home and see how Christopher did with them. It was a moment in our lives I will always remember.

I put a gate in the kitchen in order that the rabbits could not get out of the area. I would then put Christopher on the kitchen floor. He could only crawl at this time. He would get almost to the rabbits and they would hop away. He would laugh when they hopped away from him and then try again. He would do this over and over. He made me laugh. I was very thankful for the guys I worked with. They truly were a special bunch.

I became fast friends with a lot of the guys who worked on this construction site. They were all very caring, and I enjoyed my time in their presence. We had luncheons on site, and we all became like family. One guy became a regular fixture in my life for a while. Him and I bonded in a very special way. We thoroughly enjoyed our dinners together ... going to the movies ... or simply hanging out. He was married, and we never crossed any line we would be ashamed of. He became my best friend ... my shoulder to lean on. I knew he would always be there for me. He bought my son toys. He spent quality time with us. Then, as fast as we became friends, it had to end. His wife was stricken with cancer and he felt he needed to be there for her. I understood though it hurt to lose him as a part of my life. He will always be very special to me, and I think of him often. I wonder how they are doing, and I have prayed for them both often.

There was another guy on this crew who seemed to be always around. He worked for one of the subcontractors on the site, and he flirted with me a lot. Eventually he got up the nerve to ask me out for lunch. He was so cute, and I was so looking forward to dating again. I had to get back into the swing of things.

We finally went to lunch and what he shared with me shocked me to the very core. Once I recovered I only looked at it as a challenge and knew that it did not matter to me one way or the other. He told me he was a Christian. I thought to myself, "You have got to be kidding me". But, as I was so good at, I simply smiled and said it did not matter. To be honest, I did not even know what being a Christian consisted of. I just knew it would not change my way of thinking in the least, and if I did not know God by now, then I did not care to.

Tim told me what church he attended. When he did, for some reason, the name of the church set off alarms in my mind. I could not figure out why. I finally realized it was the same church my sister attended.

I called my sister to confirm this was in fact the church she attended. She confirmed it. I proceeded to ask her if she was going to attend the following Sunday. I was thinking if I went with her, then this would make me look good to Tim. I had it all planned out in my mind how this would work, but little did I know God also had it planned out how it would work.

When I shared with my sister I wanted to go to church with her, you could have bought her for a penny. Up to this point, all my family knew I wanted nothing to do with church, God, or religion. For me to say this to my sister, right out of the blue, well it left her speechless. She finally asked me what I was up to. I could not believe she said this ... LOL! She was right, of course, but I did not think I was that transparent. Eventually I shared with her why I wanted to go, and she just laughed.

I did go to church that Sunday with my sister, and I did see Tim. During the service, though I did not intend to listen to anything that was being said, something supernatural happened to me. I cannot quite explain it, but it made me want to go back the following Sunday and many Sundays after. I, of course, was in denial all along and saying Tim was the only reason I was going, but I knew it was not. I did not know what it was so how could I explain it to anyone else.

Tim and I never actually dated. We had a few lunches together. He invited me on numerous occasions to have dinner with him, but at that time, I think I was still holding out for my ex-boyfriend and I to reconcile so I never went. About a month or so of attending church, I realized it was the preaching I was enjoying. I kept going trying to figure out what all of this meant. I never ceased my drinking and partying, but I made sure I went to church on Sunday no matter how hung over I was. The people made me feel accepted and loved. They truly took an interest in me and Christopher. I was insecure enough in life where this meant something to me, and I liked how it felt. It was like nothing I had ever experienced before, and I did not want to let it go.

When I was in church, I was special. I do not know why I felt special, but I did. As soon as I entered the building, I could feel this sense of belonging in a way I never had. To make it even better, these people loved me despite who I was or what I had done. I started to reason things out. Never a good thing to do. I started telling myself the only reason they were accepting of me was because they knew nothing of me or my family. If they knew what I had done in my life, then it would be different, and they would not be so nice to me. Lies of the devil, and I was soaking them up like a sponge. Despite of all of this, I could not bring myself to stop attending.

Before I really knew what was happening, I came to know Jesus Christ personally. It was not immediate by any means, but the more I went to church, the more I found out it was the presence of the Holy Spirit I was feeling. It simply grew and grew to a point where I wanted more. Because of this intense desire, I started reading my Bible, doing my Sunday school lessons, and loving every bit of it. I was becoming truly fulfilled in a way I had never known. It was not even about the people anymore, as much as it was about Jesus.

One Sunday I dedicated my son to the Lord, and it only filled me with a desire to give myself over to Him also. I can remember the day I got saved so clearly. I had spoken to the pastor about my wanting to get saved, and it was custom at this church to allow the pastor to share with the congregation your desire. The Sunday he did this I was so excited. I went to the front of the church, and after the ceremony was over, everyone came forward to hug me and congratulate me. When Tim came through the line, I smiled at him. I can remember saying to him, "You better hug me. If it were not for you, I would not be here today". It became a joke in my family how God used a man to get me to church. I did not care what He used. I was just thankful He called me at all.

Over the course of a few months, I started to lose my desire to party and drink. I did not, by any means, just simply give it up. I fought for quite a while with my desire to party and my desire to attend church.

In time, I gave all the partying up and the desire to drink was just about gone. Eventually, I decreased my drinking and the desire to be home with my son increased daily. I still could not quite put my finger on what all of this was about, but I knew God had changed everything. He took a very damaged heart and healed it. He took a lot of negative thinking and turned it into good. He took a very insecure girl and turned her into a very secure woman. My red "X" that I had been wearing for years was finally gone. He did all of this and He did it for me.

I wish I could tell you from the moment I dedicated my life to Christ until now has been a cake walk, but I cannot. As a single mother who struggled financially, I had many difficult times in my life. On top of everything, even with all the healing He had done for me, I was still hauling around a lot of pain and scars from my past. I can tell you this though … every step of the way Jesus Christ has brought me through. He has never failed me. He has never let me down. He has always, ALWAYS loved me unconditionally. I may not have always understood the particulars of why this or that happened in my life, but I always found Him there once the confusion and fog dissipated. He has literally carried me for most of my journey, but He has also grown me up in ways only He could.

Shortly after all of this happened, I heard from Donnie yet again. We simply talked about different things. He let me know his wife and he had separated in 1989. At the time of the call, he was back living in Madison County with another lady. They shared a son together. I could sense he was not happy, but there was nothing I could do about it. The fact he called me was surely a sign he was not content with life. Otherwise why would he be calling me at all? I hung up and I could feel myself shaking. We never discussed seeing each other, and I guess I was relieved. I am not sure I would have said no, especially after finding out he was no longer with his wife. I am glad we did not arrange to see one another. I do not think it would have been good for either of us. Plus, he was involved with someone and they had a child together. It would have been so wrong on so many levels. Gosh, look at that … I have finally found my conscience.

As I did when I left my ex-husband, I lost a lot of so-called friends when I gave my life to Christ and I started living for Him. However, again, I never lost my best friend!! We were now walking on two different roads, but we loved each other too much to allow it to come between us. I had been trying to get her to church with me, but for a long time I had no success. We called each other every morning. One morning she asked me to go out with her. I made a deal with her. I told her if she would attend a Christian concert with me that I was going to in Richmond, then I would go out with her. She hesitated but she eventually agreed.

We rode together to Richmond and met up with my sister. We were going to see a Christian man by the name of Carman. I was very excited about it. I had heard him a lot on the radio and my sister raved about him a great deal. To personally see this man of God, who had dedicated his whole life to glorifying God in all he did, was a big deal for me. I was a young Christian still, and I was so excited about what God was doing in my life. The concert was great.

What was even greater though was my best friend's reaction to it all. On the way home from Richmond, she could not stop talking about Carman and the things she had witnessed that night. She said to me, "If I ever get a chance, I want my family to come the next time we see Carman, especially my niece". It spoke volumes to my heart and I was so looking forward to what I knew God could do in her life also. How perfect would it be for me now that I had the dream I had always wanted (my son), and a personal relationship with my Lord and Savior, and then to have my very best friend walking along side me? I do not think my feet were even touching ground by the time we got home. Also, get this, she said she wanted to go to church with me the following Sunday. This would be the Sunday after Thanksgiving. I suspected deep in the pit of my soul that when Carman gave out the invitation to accept the Lord as your personal savior that my very dear and precious friend did exactly that. I will never know this for a fact because as I stated earlier she died on

Thanksgiving Day. She never got to go to church with me. Later her mother shared with me how my best friend had circled the Sunday she intended to go to church with me in red on her calendar. I was truly devastated at my loss, but I am so excited at the prospect of seeing her again someday. It is a promise I have from Jesus.

The loss of my friend took a heavy toll on me. She was a part of my daily existence and I missed her so much. Over the years I would always struggle with whether she had truly given her life to Christ. I was 99% certain she had, but that 1% drove me crazy. What if she had not? What if I allowed her to leave this earth without witnessing to her personally? Thoughts of this haunted me daily.

Though life was improving by the minute, I was so lonely without my best friend. Even though I suspected she gave her heart to Christ that night so long ago, it bothered me I did not have a definitive answer. I would talk often with God about this matter. I would beg Him for confirmation. I was obsessed with knowing. God is so awesome, and He truly does know the desires of our hearts. He knew what I was struggling with internally where my best friend was concerned. He did not give me any answers immediately, but eventually He gave me the peace I needed. I received all my answers in a dream. The article I am sharing below will explain this better than I can. I wrote it after God blessed me with answers some years back.

A Dream or A Message

I lost my best friend years ago unexpectedly. Though I felt certain in the pit of my soul that she was resting in the arms of our Heavenly Father, because of the time factor involved in her death, etc., I always had a foreboding in the pit of my soul. I prayed for many years for God to show me she was with Him, so I could find complete peace. Nothing!

Since her death, I have only had one very precise dream about her and that was shortly after her death … UNTIL NOW!

Before I share this with you, I need for you to truly comprehend what her loss meant to me. I have conveyed to many on more than one occasion that if there was such a thing as a 'soul mate' where friendships were concerned, then she was my soul mate. Our relationship was far from perfect, but it was faithful and endured much. I continue to have, and in the past have had, many very special friends and even a best friend since then, but the friendship we shared was so different from any other. I never shared such a relationship with anyone prior to meeting her and I will probably never have it again.

Our loyalty to one another was evident to others as well. Though we were aware of what we shared, we were not aware that others saw it for themselves. We learned this reality one afternoon. My bestie and I were sitting in this bar drinking when another girl came over and joined us. As we sat there chatting, this other girl finally broke in and said, "I have to tell you guys that I admire your loyalty to one another. I have watched you both over the years and you are always taking care of one another. I have never witnessed such a friendship between anyone and I wish I had it." We just sort of looked at each other and chuckled.

We argued ... one day we were both very tired from working all day. She was helping me move and we had been at it for hours. We were headed to my dad's store ... me in one vehicle loaded and her following me in another vehicle full of my things. When we pulled out of my driveway, I had left either her cell phone or mine on the top of my vehicle. As we traveled down the road, she was behind me honking the horn. I just assumed she was acting crazy, which was not uncommon for either of us. We pulled in my dad's store. As we did, she jumped out of the truck and started in on me, which, of course, caused me to start in on her. I guess we did not realize how loud we were, but as my dad was coming to the front door of the store to see what all the commotion was, a customer was pulling in the driveway. My dad opened the door and said, "What in the heck is going on out here?" Before either I or she could respond, the customer said, "Earl, don't worry about it. They are just having a lover's spat." We looked at each other and just broke down laughing.

During the years of our friendship, we went through a great deal together and our loyalty would be tested more than once. There were things I said to her that I wish I could now take back, and there were things she had said to me that I knew she did not mean. It did not deter how we felt about one another.

Our constant loyalty to one another prevented her from allowing me to distance myself from her, or vice versa. Before becoming a Christian, my way of dealing with things was to lock people away and become a recluse. I was going through a 'pity party' and had been held up in my house, feeling sorry for myself, for about 2 days. I would not answer the phone or return calls. One morning as I was just waking up, I heard my front door open. You could tell by the way the door opened and the heaviness of the person's walk that they were on a mission. Before I could gather my thoughts, my bedroom door flew open, and she said, "If you think you are going to avoid me forever and just sit here feeling sorry for yourself, you are crazy." She proceeded to crawl in the bed with me. As she did, she looked at me and said, "We can feel sorry for ourselves together." Again, we started to laugh, and as normal, it was over. This is just the way we were with each other.

When I gave my life to Christ, though we were walking on different trails, we still spoke every morning and were there for each other. About a year after my conversion, I talked her into going to a Christian concert with me. It was then that I knew without a doubt that she had given her life to Christ. She could not stop talking about the concert all the way home. She anxiously told me that she was going to church with me soon. Unfortunately, 'soon' never came as the Lord called her home.

In sharing the above, I hope you can truly grasp the significance of this dream:

I was sitting on a park bench and I had my head in my hands crying. As I was sitting there, I could feel someone put their arms around my shoulders and sit down next to me. As I lifted my head to see who it was, it became apparent to me that it was her.

At first, I was a bit startled and just stared at her. The longer I stared the more I could feel this anger seeping within. I sort of slid away from her and I said through my tears, "Why did you leave me? Now I have no one to talk to and I feel all alone. I don't know what to do with all of this hurt over things in my life. I do not understand why people we loved have distanced themselves from me. I do not understand why people think I am a Christian fanatic. Why do people want to hurt me when all I want to do is help them? Why do people want to talk about me behind my back? You are not here to reassure me, and I am alone."

She reached over and wiped the tears from my eyes. Very tenderly she said, "Janet, you are never alone, and I did not leave you. I am with you every day. I know things are not as they were, but I can tell you that you are exactly who you should and need to be. Do you remember when you used to tell me all the time not to allow what others thought of me to define who I was, and how if they did not accept the love I had, then it was their loss? Well, now I am saying the same thing to you. Do not ever change what you are doing or who you are. It is touching lives even though you do not always get to see it. I love you and I am always right here beside you. However, listen to me! I need to share something with you. I am not making light of what you are going through at this moment, but this is not why I am here with you. I came to thank you and to show you that what you do does matter as it changed my life. You allowed God to use you to save me from living eternity in hell. If it were not for your persistence and love, I would not be in heaven today. I would be spending my eternity in pain and suffering. Don't you see … you loved me enough to be honest with me no matter what I said. You cared more about me than you did about what I thought of you. You saved my life and you are saving other people's lives also. Please, take my word for this. As for people we loved hurting you or whatever, I do not know what to say. It confuses me, and it is not as I would want it to be. I simply do not have the capacity to think of such things. In heaven, I have nothing but joy in my heart. I am not suffering with all the issues I had when here on earth. I am happy."

As I looked at her, she just radiated with happiness and she looked so young. I said to her, "Don't you miss me and everyone else?" She replied, "Again, I do not have the capacity to deal with such issues. Heaven is just about being happy and loving God. I am spending time with your mom and dad, and with other people I know. It is wonderful, and I have you to thank for this … you and our Heavenly Father."

I started to cry again. I said to her, "It is unfair that you left me. I need you here." She responded in a very stern but loving voice, "Janet, listen to me. My time was done here and yours is not. Do you remember the vision God gave you a few months back? Well it is not fulfilled yet? (I sat in shock with my mouth opened as I was not aware she knew about this vision.) Please, just listen to me. You are not alone. I am watching over you, but more importantly, God is watching over you. He has great things in store for you. Just do not change no matter what others say, no matter what they do not say, or what they do to you. Keep your eyes focused on Him."

As she was saying this, she was beginning to fade. I reached out to stop her from leaving, and she said, "I have to go but more importantly I want to go. If given the chance, I would not return. I would not give up this sense of peace and happiness I now have for anyone. I love you. I am always with you, and oh yeah, this should make you happy ... your son and daughter love you and cannot wait to meet you. Good bye my friend."

As quickly as she came, she left. When I woke from my dream, I felt such a peace within. I knew without a doubt I had been visited by my friend. Now as for me crying and being upset, I do not know what that was all about. I am struggling with a few things in my life but nothing as dramatic as this dream seemed to convey. I am a bit disillusioned by some people in my life, but I guess she knew something I do not yet know. Some of the things she shared with me made total sense and some left me wondering. I know there is a message

here for me, and I will pray God reveals it to me.
However, I so enjoyed our short visit. It did not
leave me longing for more, but thankful for what we
had.

There is a lesson to be had in all of this, for me and you. We often hear the words 'don't take today for granted'. It is so true. If you are a Christian, share your faith with others. Share your testimony of what God has done in your life to give them hope. Tomorrow may be too late. Writing this book has been so very difficult for me. I only put myself through it because it could very well speak to the heart of another. I may never know for certain, but what I do know for certain is that God has a reason for me to put myself through this. I trust Him!

Chapter Twenty

For the next ten years, I would be a single mother simply raising my son and basking in the love I had found in Christ. It was ten years of growing in ways I never had before. Though I went through some horrendous times of testing, I would not change a thing. I became independent. I became responsible. I learned things I should have been taught earlier in life. It was truly a time of one-on-one with Christ. Those ten years in the desert, totally by myself except for the love of Christ, were the best and worse times of my life. I did not date and I was happy to be without a man. God had brought me a very long way and I never wanted to look back. No matter what life threw at me and believe me when I say life threw a lot, it could never measure up to what I had found in Him.

By now it was 2007. One day a family member and I were on our way out of town. My whole family has been amazed at the changes in my life. During our trip, this individual asked me what was the one thing I feared could hamper my walk with Christ? Without even thinking, I blurted out Donnie's name. I knew if Donnie was ever to return, I would struggle immensely with meeting him again. I had not heard from him in about seven years, and the last time we had contact was strictly over the telephone. He had called me at my job and we simply talked. It left me with an emptiness inside, but not a void as it had always been. I had realized that the void I had in my life had nothing to do with my anger or bitterness. The void was not having a personal relationship with my God. We are all created with that void in our lives, and sadly for some, they never figure this out. You hear all the time of people who have riches, beauty, and everything they could possibly desire. Yet, they are still unfulfilled. It is simply because they were created for God's purpose, and without Him in our lives, we never feel completely fulfilled.

Two weeks after I made that trip, I was home one evening sitting at the kitchen table when my telephone rang. It was my sister calling from my dad's home. She said to me, *"You will never guess who just called here looking for you."* I did not need to guess, I responded, *"Donnie"*. I was correct. He wanted her to give him my home telephone number, but of course, she would not. She did, however, get his cell phone number so I could call him.

I hung up and the butterflies in my stomach were all over the place. You would have thought by now the mention of his name would not affect me like this, but it did. I know I was smiling from ear to ear. I waited about ten or fifteen minutes and then I called him.

We both agreed we wanted to see each other again. We did not make a date at that time, and we left it where he would get back in touch with me. I could not sleep that night. As I laid in bed I relived so much of my life, and as I did, it made me appreciate my life with Christ even more. It also felt good to know that when and if Donnie and I were to meet, this time it would be with a clean conscience. No spouses were involved. and I would not be hurting anyone.

A few days after we originally spoke on the telephone, we agreed to meet at a local restaurant in Charlottesville. Was I nervous? I could hardly believe this was happening. Though it had been years since we spoke, it was even longer since we had seen one another. I shared with the girls at work whom I was going to meet, and we were like high school girls laughing and being all silly. It was fun, and it only intensified the time between then and when we would meet.

I drove to the restaurant and parked in the lot. I had forgotten to ask Donnie what he was driving, but he knew what I was driving. As I was sitting there waiting, I needed to make sure that every hair was in place and I looked as good as I could. I prayed a silent prayer of thanksgiving to God and asked Him to carry me through this time. I was about as nervous as anyone could be, but I was also very excited. I could not believe I was 50 years of age and still felt the same. I could honestly say that on some level I was still in love with the boy I met at the age of 13. We had traveled many roads together and apart.

I finally spotted him in my rearview mirror. As much as I wanted to get out of my van and meet him, my legs would not move. He approached the passenger side of my vehicle and got in. We both simply looked at each other and smiled. Once the initial shock had worn off, we exited the van and walked back to his vehicle. We stood there and chatted for a while, and he told me he could tell I was very nervous. How could I not be? Then he leaned in and kissed me. I thought my knees would buckle right then and there, but they did not. We chatted for a bit longer and then I told him I had to get home to my son. He kissed me again, and when I was walking away, he said, "*I wish I could put you in my PT Cruiser and take you home and take care of you*". I thought it was the sweetest thing anyone had ever said to me.

This was the beginning of many, many dates. I cannot say that it was all smooth sailing because it was not. We simply dated on and off for a few months, and then we eventually called it quits. He had a lot of unresolved issues in his life, and it appeared as if it simply would not work out. We did not see each other for nine months.

In April of 2008, Donnie would show up on my doorstep once again. This time we were ready to make a commitment to one another. It had been a long haul, but we had finally cleared out all the junk in our lives to a point where we could focus on just us.

During this time, I thought about my mom a great deal. I wondered how she would feel about all of this. As with most girls, I wanted so desperately to share this special time in my life with her. She had gone home to be with the Lord. Daddy was still with us, but he was struggling with Alzheimer's. For a few years, my son and I lived with daddy to take care of him, but eventually it became more than I could handle. Donnie spent time with me at daddy's house, but we always wondered if he truly knew who Donnie was. Part of me says no, but then I will never know for certain.

Even from the onset in 2007, once Donnie and I started to seriously date, I did not consult God in any of this. How do I explain this to you? When Donnie came back, it was as if a part of me became thirteen again. I did not see him as the man he was today, but in my warped way of thinking, he was the 17-year-old boy who loved me compassionately and would do anything for me. It was on these feelings that I made all my decisions. Though I was still walking with Christ and living my life for Him, I unintentionally put Him in second place and put my relationship with Donnie in first. I did things I should not have done, and I behaved in ways I should not have. I am not very proud of this. I know people reading this will wonder how I could have even done this if I had such a wonderful and strong relationship with Christ. I cannot give you an easy answer. I guess I was partially living in a dream world … a dream I had carried around with me for over 40+ years. I was not about to jeopardize it now. I had a second chance. In my twisted thinking, God was blessing me with what only He could give me … He was restoring to me what others had robbed me of. There were many signs I should have paid attention to, but I refused to heed any advice. There were many warnings about difficulties that lied ahead, but I refused to acknowledge them. I was not going to allow anyone or anything to take Donnie away from me again. I should have trusted all of this to Christ. I should have known if this was God's plan for me then He would have handled it, but I would not even allow myself to think this way. I was determined this time to see it through to the end.

Donnie and I dated for a little over a year, and we got married on October 9, 2009. As you can well imagine, it was a very emotional day for both of us. It was not the church wedding I had always envisioned for us ... I did not wear the traditional white wedding dress ... and I did not get to walk down that aisle knowing the man of my dreams was waiting for me. It was a simple day at the Justice of the Peace, but it was years in the making. It was a day we tried to bring about twice before. It was a day we never thought we would live to see. During our nuptials, emotions would finally take over and we both began crying.

Also, it was a very special day not only because we got married, but because my beautiful daughter was born on the same day. For any reasons, we never told anyone we were getting married. We simply slipped away and did it. I did, however, have my best friend's mother go with me to share this day. I could not have my best friend, so at least I could have the next best thing. On top of everything else, her mother had just lost her husband and I wanted to bring some joy into her life.

As we stood together taking our vows, I could not help but think about my parents. I was so sad my dad was now in a nursing home, and Alzheimer's had well taken his mind. I would have given anything for him to be there for me. The absence of my mother was even harder. I know she would have been so happy to finally see this day. I think it would have brought her a much-needed peace of mind. Nevertheless, I know she was looking down from Heaven and clapping her hands as only she could. It truly brought tears to my eyes, but for once in my life they were tears of joy and not sadness.

We eventually shared the news with our families and we got mixed reviews. However, I can tell you this ... my family was very happy for us. They all knew what this day meant to me. My sister gave us a small reception at her home a few days later, and I was one happy girl. After thirty-seven years, we had found our way back together and we were finally husband and wife after two failed attempts. What is it that they say, "*The 3rd time's a charm*"?

Our first year of marriage was a difficult one. I think after we moved in together we realized we were not 13 and 17. We were not those kids anymore. I was looking to Donnie for all the things he supplied when I was younger. Though I did not really need those things, it was who I was expecting. Donnie had also been through a lot over the years which had changed him a great deal. Twenty years of serving his country, along with other events, had affected his life in big ways. We both had changed, and now we had to get to know each other all over again. As Christ was and is always with me, we have managed to survive. As we enter our 6th year of marriage, things have improved immensely. I do not for one second regret my decision as I love my husband very much.

Since marrying, Donnie and I have discussed our younger years and I have realized a few things I did not know. One thing that he shared with me which had the greatest impact the most was how his mother truly felt about my pregnancy. During that time and all these years later, I just assumed she hated me, and I was never good enough in her eyes. This was not how she felt at all. Donnie said she was very excited at the prospect of having another grandchild and she was very happy we would be living with her. He said when it all came to a head and there was no more pregnancy that his mom was very sad and hurt. I wish I had known this as I would have gone to her. It would have made our trip to Richmond all those years earlier a bit easier.

As for Donnie's dad, when we married he was married to another lady as Donnie's mom had passed years prior to us marrying. I wanted on more than one occasion to speak to him about that period in our lives, especially since I would sit beside his bed at the nursing home during his final years. I could never bring myself to do it. Donnie's dad did not believe in divorce. Though Donnie and his wife separated in 1989, they never legally divorced even though Donnie had another life with someone else, with whom he shared a son. In order for Donnie and I to marry, he had to divorce his first wife. I knew this was not to Donnie's dad's liking, so it always kept me a bit intimidated around him. I allowed fear to win out when I should not have. I have many regrets, but they are all in the past now. I truly live for today and the many blessings that I have.

God has truly blessed my life beyond my wildest dreams. I am only sorry I did not give my life to Him sooner, or at least allow Him to speak to me. I wonder sometimes where I would be today if I had been raised in a Christian home. But, you know what, none of that matters. I have come to know I had to walk the road I did to truly appreciate where God has brought me from.

I know my abortion altered my life and set a course for destruction from that moment on. It was not an easy solution for a problem. I simply do not know how people could say that it is. Setting aside the biblical aspects of an abortion, this action in one's life is destructive. I can say this because I have lived it. I killed my own flesh and blood. Yes, I was young, and I had no control over my actions. This does not make it any less painful. I am not sure I would have done it differently if it was me that had made the decision and not my parents. I just know I walk in total forgiveness today without all the pain and scars I hauled around for so long, from one relationship to another, from one day to another. None of that will ever change the fact that I have two precious children in heaven today … James Michael and Sarah Renee. I am excited at the prospect of meeting them and spending eternity with them.

I also am so thankful for my two precious children I have today. I could not imagine my life without either of them. My daughter is a wonderful person whom I love with all my heart. My three grandsons are so special to me. And then, there is Christopher. He truly was a blessing from heaven and a most precious gift from a very special person. How much more special could it be!

My son has and continues to be my inspiration in life. He attends a Christian school. He dedicated his life to Christ when he was in elementary school. The day he called me on the telephone from school to share this news with me, I was ecstatic. I had told myself I would introduce him to Christ as he grew up, but whether to have that personal relationship with Christ would have to be his decision. Previously, in the public elementary school that Christopher attended, once a week some people held a group gathering entitled "The Good News Club". It was in no way affiliated with the school. It was during one of these group gatherings that my precious son surrendered his life to Christ. I thank God for that every day. It truly brings peace and comfort to my heart to know Christopher is seeking the will of the Lord for his life also. It does not mean he will not have trials growing up, but I can rest in God's Word in Proverbs 22:6 which states: *"Train up a child in the way he should go, and when he is old, he will not depart from it". NKJ* It is not a guarantee Christopher will not go down some difficult roads in his life, but it is a promise from God he will return to Christ before it is over. I can rest easy knowing this.

My daughter is a blessing all her own. She is married to a wonderful man today who has been a true hero to her and my grandsons. They have weathered storms of their own and come out ahead. They have a great future together, and I am blessed beyond words. They are also attending church and it warms my heart to no end.

Chapter Twenty-One

Though I have my awesome personal relationship with Christ, it does not deter difficulties in life. We all want what is best and to be happy. It is not our goal in life to have less. I have found that if we do not seek His will for our lives and strive to walk with Him daily then less is exactly what we get.

As of the writing of this book (the beginning of 2018), Donnie and I are legally separated. Try as we did, there simply were too many obstacles for us to overcome. Each day brought challenges anew and we ran out of steam for the battle. We were not 13 and 17 any longer.

At thirteen, I was solely reliant upon Donnie for so much. I was insecure, so I clung to him in ways which were truly unhealthy. I was now very independent and a bit strong willed. I had toughened quite a bit during my ten years in the desert. I was not used to having to answer to anyone except God, and He even had battles with me. I think I still carried a lot of resentment deep on the inside of me towards Donnie which I would not come to realize until later. There was a lot of water under the bridge, and there was a lot of unresolved pain.

Donnie, on the other hand, had been through a lot and he was not the same as I had known him. During our years apart, he had endured his own life struggles. Instead of us coming together to grow, we entered a battle zone of our own making. In our early years of marriage, Donnie had no relationship with Christ, but he would come to know Him a few years prior to our separation.

Take all the above and throw in five stepchildren, along with my children, and you have a situation sort of like the one my parents had. Everyone had their own issues and feelings about our marriage. We had a history which was not pleasant to all involved. It was a mess we tried to ignore. You can only wear blinders for so long before you run into a brick wall.

Today, Donnie and I are once again striving to work things out. Though we still reside in separate homes, we love each other too much to throw in the towel just yet. We are living apart, but we are reconciled and building a new future ... one brick at a time. We have a strong foundation in love and in Christ, so I am praying the rest will take care of itself. We could use all the prayers you have.

I am convinced it is God's will for Donnie and I to be together. I am just not sure we allowed things to work out in His timing. I think we got ahead of the plan, and thus our hardships.

God has a design for all our lives. He has a chosen path He wants us to walk. I feel certain in my heart that Donnie and I being together was His design. I am not so sure it was to happen when we choose it to happen. I am confident we put the cart before the horse.

I sense had Donnie and I waited for His timing, then all the healing and work which needed to be done in and through us by Him would have been manifested. We would have met being healthy and strong in our walk with Christ. Instead, we got ahead of ourselves and came in the midst of His cleansing. Therefore, we are going to have to walk through the storms and weather the strong winds. It is going to take faith, hope, and sole reliance upon Him. I pray we are up for the challenge, but only time will tell. I do know it is not God's design that we should divorce.

Donnie and I have a lot to overcome, not only between us but with outside sources, and within one another personally. Time does not heal everything. God is at work and I trust Him completely. I start my day with Him, I think of Him every second of every day, and I end my day with Him on my mind. I am completely and utterly reliant upon Him for all things. Our battles are many, but our Protector is more than ready if we will only give it over to Him. This does not mean each day will be sunshine and roses, but it is our guarantee we can weather the storms. Each storm we overcome only strengthens us for the next, and believe me, there will always be torrential downpours to endure. You cannot live without them. It is impossible!!

As I previously shared, my experience in life effected so many around me. I could not properly tell you how. I pondered different ways to do just that during this process. After much prayer, God placed it upon my heart to ask some of my siblings to share what they remembered about my abortion. Below are the letters they shared with me for this book. Though I have typed them for insertion in this book, I have not changed what they wrote.

Letter from my sister, Cathy:

Dear Readers:

When Janet had her abortion, I was too little to know what was happening, so I can't remember how it may have affected me then. But I do know how it affected me later in life, many years later.

I remember watching Janet as she held other babies; it was always such a bitter sweet event. She would stare at them with such love, but you could see the hurt in her eyes because she did not have her own baby to hold.

Janet never had her own child by natural birth, but she is a MOTHER to many. She always took on that Motherly role.

Later when I got married and decided to have children of my own, I remember not wanting to hurt her by my becoming pregnant. I will never forget when I lost my first baby during the early months of pregnancy, Janet stayed right by my side, but her pain seemed much greater than mine.

Later when I was able to get pregnant again and did give birth to my first healthy baby boy, again Janet was there. It was such a bittersweet moment. You knew she was so happy for me, but it also seemed to bring sadness to her.

So, I guess Janet's abortion did not affect me directly, but it did steal away some joy from my sister that never returned and as hard as I tried, I could never fully understand. It always broke my heart because I love her very much.

With Love,

Cathy Rogers

Below is the letter from my sister, Virginia:

To Whom It May Concern: I can't really remember exactly when it was that I realized that Janet had an abortion. I was too young to have remembered anything and it was not something we would have been discussed in our family. Janet and I had a rather close relationship in our younger years but never to the point of talking about something so personal.

There was an age gap between us and I was more like her shadow then a good friend.

I remember sometime in my early adult life that Janet had a lot of medical problems and was struggling getting pregnant. It was sometime than that I either put the pieces together or overheard something that made me realize this was why she was having so many problems. I still remember the day she found out she was pregnant; and worse yet the day we found out she had miscarried. It was hard on Janet and the family. From that point forward, it seemed that babies and being pregnant was a closed subject.

Many years later my younger sister went on to have my nephew, I remember having conversations with her about her pregnancy and how it affected Janet. Sometimes it was like walking on eggshells. It wasn't that Janet would say anything, but you could tell by her demeanor that it hurt her.

Over the years Janet and I had drifted apart and though nothing had really happen between us it seemed that there was an invisible wedge between us. We still had good times when we were together, but it always appeared to be that "White Elephant" in the room. I loved my sister very much and never could really figure out why we struggled so hard with our relationship.

A couple years later I became pregnant with my daughter, Angela. It was a exciting time for my husband and I but I remember so clearly the heaviness that came over me when I realized I had to tell my big sister I was pregnant. How would she react? Would this finally be the one thing that would totally destroy us? I remember having so many fixed emotions; excitement, sadness and anger. It was so mentally exhausting. I wanted to be happy but how could I when this was going to hurt my sister so badly.

Finally, that day came. We were all at mom's house. I don't really remember the occasion, maybe Thanksgiving, but everyone was there, and I wanted to share my big news. I had decided I was going to tell Janet first, so I called her in one of the back bedrooms. I still remember telling her that I had something to say but I was so scared she was going to hate me. I started crying before I even got the words out. As any good big sister would do, she put her arms around me and told me it was okay, and to just tell her what was going on. So I did. I knew at that moment that she didn't hate me. She was truly happy for me. There was one thing she would ask of me and that was if it was a girl to name it after her best friend who had been killed in a car accident. **(Note from Janet: My friend, the first I met who was with me when I met Donnie was killed shortly after I married my ex-husband. It was a difficult time for me. She is always in my heart, and I will never forget our friendship.)**

That day was a big stepping stone for us. I remember feeling like a huge weight had been lifted off me. Although things got better, and we moved forward, it was always there in the back of all of our minds. We always seemed to keep baby conversations and the excitement that came with it down to a minimum. How could we not.

Sincerely,

Virginia Johnston

This third and last letter is the one that truly spoke volumes to me. I cannot believe what my baby brother shared, and it simply blows my mind how something so trivial to some can catapult to such dimensions in the life of another.

Dear Janet,

Ok, let me give it a shot. I'm not the writer I use to be. I do more thinking then writing.

Anyway, you ask how you getting an abortion affected me growing up. Well my memory isn't what it used to be. I don't know if you remember me even bringing it up or writing you a letter some years ago about this very subject. But I did.

Sis, I don't know if you remember it or not or what I wrote you about this subject. But it went something like this. Hell, I don't know how old I was, but a kid. I think I was in your room and I found a letter you apparently wrote Donnie or somebody. Being nosy, reading it, I came to a word I did not know. (I think!) It is how I remember it in my head anyway over the years. So, I ask mom what the word was. She snatched the letter from me – read it, and she took off to the phone. I knew (felt) I had done something wrong.

Like I said, Sis, my memory isn't what it used to be. Now, it is more of a story in my mind and heart then a memory.

I think you went away shortly thereafter. Somewhere along the line or during this time I found out you were pregnant – maybe I put 2 and 1 together – I don't know. All I remember 'very clearly' is listening and keeping quiet about it. I knew that letter started whatever was going on and I was scared.

These aren't good memories for me, Sis, and I'm going to give you the short version.

I kept that letter to myself. I never told anyone until I wrote you that letter from prison in Florida. But as the years ticked on – we did a lot of things together. Mostly a lot of drinking and partying. And many, many times in our drunken state – you'd cry on my shoulder, or shared with me your feelings about the abortion, not being able to have children, Donnie, mom and dad, etc. And I'd cry right with you. Feeling so sad, so guilty for that letter, and sometimes I'd run away later that night. I remember one time running away and stealing a car, and you later asking me why I do such things as that? And I just wanted to tell you then how sorry I was – that it was all my fault. But I couldn't. I was scared you'd hate me. I felt that way from the moment I found that letter – even now kinda sorta as I write this. But not like before. I always felt guilty and that it was my fault. I can literally talk about it today without crying uncontrollable – but I still feel the sadness writing this and a tear or two.

Remember, Sis – I did not write you that letter until I was in my 30's. And I was scared to death. I was in that drug program in Florida prison. Dade Correctional Institute. From the day I found that letter until the day I wrote you that letter – I would had rather died then for anyone (especially you) to know I was the one who put the wheels in motion to the biggest tragedy of your lifetime.

Anyway, Sis, there you have it. A very short version. I can't believe you got this out of me. I am much better these days at avoiding feelings – especially painful ones. And believe me when I say this.

Janet, your abortion and that letter in the mind of a child – the guilt I carried – it all had a profound effect on me. I loved my big sister. And I feared if she knew, I'd lose her. From childhood to adulthood! I love you, Sis, for what it's worth and I am sorry.

Love Jimbo

As I read his letter, I cried uncontrollably at what he carried all these years and what he believed he had done. He was simply an innocent child who had nothing to do with anything. He snuck into his older sister's bedroom, found a letter, and like any little boy took it to his mom. I am thinking that the letter addressed the possibility of me being pregnant. What I do not understand is why my mom rushed to the telephone, etc. Now I must wonder if Donnie told my parents or Jimmy did inadvertently. When I arrived home that day after being summoned from my friend's house, did Donnie get summoned too? Did he simply arrive before me? I do not know, and to be honest, Donnie cannot remember. We have discussed it but our memories are not completely the same. It is, however, sad that this young boy took this guilt into his manhood and never got release from it until now.

I did not seek letters from my two older brothers. One is in the early stages of Parkinson's and my other was not really around much when this occurred. I am sure they have memories and thoughts pertaining to this part of my life. I am sure it affected them in some ways. I just did not feel inclined to get them to write a letter. I hope neither find this offensive in any way. They are my big brothers and the roles they played in my life were special to me then and always will be. I am proud to call them brothers!

It is over. This is my testimony. I do not know where it will lead or what direction it will take my life, but I do know without any doubt, my life truly has come full circle. I have managed to **forgive but I will never forget the journey, or the lessons learned!**

Forgiven ... But Never Forgotten

-

"Forgiven ... But Never Forgotten" was originally the title for this book. It was exactly how I felt until someone showed me the other side of this title. To me "Forgiven" was for those and myself who I held bitterness towards in my heart. It was my way of saying I had forgiven all involved and I was letting go. The "But Never Forgotten" was for my two precious children in heaven. I have never forgotten them, nor shall I.

Running the title together, "Forgiven ... But Never Forgotten" was being interpreted by others as my forgiving people but not forgetting what they had done. In presenting this to me, my younger brother said to me, *"Sis, isn't that contrary to what God says? We are to forgive completely. God forgave our sins as far as the east is from the west so what right do we have to forgive others but remember their sins?"* This is what people thought I was referring to with the title "Forgiven ... But Never Forgotten". Hence, the title was changed to *"My Story".*

Sometimes in life we can completely deceive ourselves into thinking we have forgiven people when in fact we have not. Unforgiveness is a horrible thing to carry around. We think we are in control of our feelings when we carry the unforgiveness, but it is quite the opposite. When we choose to not forgive others, it is giving them the control. The unforgiveness rules our hearts, our minds, and our actions. As it grows on the inside of us daily, it manifests itself in very destructive ways.

Take my half-siblings for example. Look at how their unforgiveness and bitterness at the demise of their mother and our father's divorce carried over towards us. The children born out of my parent's union are innocent to anything which occurred before our birth. Yet, it was we that received the bulk of their unforgiveness for years upon years and still to this day. The bitterness they harbor towards us has been very destructive in their lives whether they are able to acknowledge this or not. It rules them and has carried over into aspects of their own personal lives.

I once dated a guy who carried a lot of bitterness deep on the inside of him. He was bitter over his childhood ... he was bitter over his life ... he was bitter over a failed marriage ... he was bitter over relationships with siblings. To meet this individual out in public, you would come away thinking he was the sweetest person you ever met. However, as I got to know him personally, you could see where he wore his bitterness upon his sleeve. It comes out against situations and people entirely innocent of anything that may have occurred in his life. It is very sad!

Bitterness and anger are spoken about a great deal in the Bible. God cautions us many times about the havoc they can cause. More importantly, if you have any unforgiveness in your heart, then God does not heed your prayers.

We as Christians have been forgiven for the greatest of offenses. God forgave us when we knowingly sinned against Him. There is nothing man has done to us or can do to us which would measure up to how we have sinned against God. In Mark 11:25 (NKJ) Jesus says, "And whenever you stand praying, forgive, if you have anything against anyone, so that your Father also who is in heaven may forgive you your trespasses." If you refuse to do this, then God does not hear your prayers.

I can tell you firsthand how I was robbed of so much joy in my life because of the bitterness I harbored on the inside. I lost a lot of precious years enjoying the happiest times of my sisters' lives. I missed out on their baby showers. I put a wall between us. At a time when we should have been bonding and rejoicing in new life, I was angry and unable to do so. Who do you think this hurt? Yes, it hurt them in their heart, but it did not hinder their joy or their ability to enjoy those special times. It was me who missed out. It is time I can never get back. What are you missing out on today? It is your choice to forgive or not to forgive, the same as it was mine.

Thank you, baby bro, for the input!!!!

Acknowledgements

I purposely waited to put the acknowledgements section of this book last. Had I put it where it initially goes, then you ... my readers ... would have learned more of the story beforehand than you should have. It would have taken away from the book. Therefore, I put the acknowledgements at the end instead of at the beginning.

In Memory of My Mom

Janice Elizabeth Molton
January 7, 1932 – September 17, 2004

As you can see from the picture above, my mom was not only beautiful on the inside, but she was beautiful on the outside as well. It would be her inner beauty that touched the lives of many. It is only fitting I dedicate this book to the woman who gave me birth. Her presence in my life is missed every day.

My mom went home to be with the Lord a little over thirteen years ago. There have been many times since I knew I was to write this book that I have longed to speak with her about it. I would give anything to have her feedback. Now that I am here I realize I need to dedicate this book to her memory. There is no doubt in my mind that had abortion been available at any time during my mother's child-bearing years, she would never have opted for it. She would have struggled and done whatever was necessary to sacrifice for her unborn child. Knowing this has caused me bitterness and a lack of understanding why the decisions that were made for me happened at all. The conviction in my heart of how precious life was to my mother when it came to her children has confused me throughout this process. The inability to speak with her about this left me in turmoil during periods of writing this book. The void her death has left in my heart can never be expressed in words.

For you to truly know the person my mom was and what she meant to her family, I would have to write a separate book. Obstacles would not elude her in life, but her perseverance would amaze many.

Though wealth and prosperity would be evident in the families of some of her distant relatives, my mom was raised in poverty. Her young life, as well as her adult life, would be altered by alcoholism, mental illness, physical abuse, sexual abuse, and these just to name a few. As an adult, she would strive so desperately to overcome the effects these things had on her life, but it would only be coupled with rheumatoid arthritis and numerous other medical issues which would eventually lead to her death at an early age. I can only imagine what impact her trials in life left on her heart and soul.

My mom was a fighter. She loved life and she fought hard for every breath she took. Her children and husband were her lifeline, and as long as she had us, she could overcome obstacles most only hear about. Many, many times she would be in the hospital and the doctors would not give us much hope; however, she would overcome and return home to us. She tried as best she could to teach us we could be anything we wanted to be. She believed in hard work. Yet her desire to make life easier for her children than it had been for her and my dad would hinder our growth immensely in years to come and hamper the lessons we all benefit and learn from doing hard work.

At times in my life, I would struggle with anger at my parents for making my life too easy. It would make it difficult for me to truly grasp the words "*you can do anything if you work hard*" when they worked so hard to make things as simple for me as they could. I still struggle with the mixed messages I received growing up. Being a parent myself, I can understand how easy it is for us as parents to go overboard in protecting our children. I pray through the grace of God that He always reminds me we have to let our children fall in order that they learn how to get back up. Discipline only lasts for a minute, but the lack of it lasts for a lifetime.

I would fall many times in my life, but it would be God who taught me to get up. It was not an easy concept after 40+ years of falling and not knowing how to get back up, but we truly do serve a God of miracles.

My mom's many hardships throughout her life would deprive us of the relationship we should have had. Somehow over the course of time I became very protective of my mom. I would sacrifice parts of my life trying to make hers better. To be totally honest with you and myself, I know now that what I really was doing was trying to make up for some of the pain I had brought her.

I know my mom loved me as much as a mother could. We had a very confusing relationship and she would be one of the main reasons I struggled so much in writing this book. I could not get pass the fact that I needed so much to speak with her. I wondered how she would feel about what I was doing. After all, this was something we never discussed. It happened. It was taken care of. It was forgotten, or so we thought! I lived a life of constant conflict and many years of torment because of the decisions which were made, and I have come to know that my family, especially my mom, did not go untouched by what happened to me. It may have been buried, but it was never forgotten … just never spoken of.

I would learn over the years through conversations, tidbits of gossip, acts, and many ways how this one decision affected the lives of many more than just me … *my siblings, my parents, myself, and in the years to come, my own family*. I hurt so much because I so desperately needed to seek the guidance of my mom in order to move forward. I wrestled with this continually. One day God said, *"Write her a letter"* and so I did.

Dear Mom:

For many years I have struggled with who I was and where I belonged in this world. I could never quite figure out why I was here and what my life was about. I had this emptiness in the pit of my gut that could never be filled, so I searched in all the wrong places for the answers.

You and dad made a decision for me many years ago. I wonder now if you could have known firsthand the effect it had on my life, and the lives of others, would you have done it? Knowing it would forever haunt each of us, would you have chosen a different route?

The day I returned home from the hospital, it was final. It was never spoken of again. I truly thought it was behind us. Well, obviously, this was never the case or I would not be writing this book. It was not the case with you either, Mom. The guilt you carried around for years would fester in your very soul, the same way it was festering in mine. How sad that we never could find the safe place we both needed in order to comfort each other and help cleanse us both. You could not come to me, and I hid it so deep in my soul that I did not think I needed to come to anyone. Unfortunately, I would learn of your pain through others. The relationship you had with my younger sisters would allow you to share this with them. How sad we did not have the same.

Over the years, I would hear second hand of your guilt. You would think in knowing this I would have been encouraged to come to you. I simply could not bring myself to do that. To come to you would mean I would have to deal with it, and since I did not think it was an issue, then why bring it up?

Mom, God has brought it up. After giving my life to Him, He has been working on getting me to this very place. He has given me the ability to use our suffering to reach the hearts of others. I allowed you to go through life thinking I had not forgiven you. Oh, how I hate that I allowed that to happen. If I could take it back, I would. If I had known where this was leading, I would have come to you, Mom. Knowing you suffered in silence when I could have alleviated some of your pain and torment breaks my heart.

Mom, God has given me the opportunity to make it right for both of us. Though you are not here, you are my inspiration to press on. I have to believe you are hearing these words. I can picture you smiling down on me. I feel your loving arms around me. I hear your words of encouragement.

I know without a doubt you would approve of this book. Though we were raised constantly hearing "what would the neighbors think," I have to believe we learned to get past that. I heard that saying any time there were issues in our home. I heard it so much I abhorred it. I almost allowed those very words to turn my back on what God has been trying to do in me … I used it as an excuse many times to not write this book. Each time I felt the Lord would lay this on my heart, I would think, "How will this effect so and so? What will the people that know me think? What will my family say? How will the people in the church perceive me after this?" Well, Mom, no more! I am doing this for you and for me, but more importantly, because God knows I have something valuable that needs to be shared. I have an opportunity to use my pain in order to save someone else from making the same mistakes I did in life … maybe help another set of parents who read my story not do the same with their teenage daughter … maybe help a boyfriend realize that sex is not a way of showing love at that age and it is a precious gift from God for the pleasure of a husband and wife.

Mom, I have forgiven you, and I ask you do the same for me. I should have known your love for me would enable me to overcome anything. You needed me just as much as I needed you, but the concept of shoving the problem under the rug was stronger than my courage to come to you. It just was not talked about, nor was any major problems in our family. This was not your fault, Mom. I know this now. You were just passing down the way you were taught.

I am so thankful for having you as my mom. You were the best, and if I can be half the mom to my children that you were to me, then I will have blessed them. I may not have always agreed with the decisions you made, but God has shown me that you gave your best at that given time. It is not what I would hope to give my children, but it was all you had. You were thinking of me when you and dad made the decisions you did. I know that now. I am going to make many mistakes in rearing my son, and God knows, I already made my fair share in raising my daughter. I pray that someday they both will come to the same conclusion God has shared with me … knowing I gave my all at that given time. It was my best, just as you and dad gave me your best. Our best may not always be their best, or even what is right, but it is what we thought was right at the time.

I am so thankful you went home to be with the Lord knowing in your heart my life had changed. I am sorry for all I ever put you through. The unconditional love you gave everyone has left its mark … you have touched the lives of many and you continue to do so. People are taught today to measure prosperity in monetary terms … in the size of their home … in the car they drive and so on. Well, Mom, you were rich in love and others are enriched because of the love you gave them. Everyone who attended your funeral could attest to this. They came out in droves to honor a woman who truly touched lives and who was rich in love. If I can do the same through this book, then I will die as wealthy a woman as you did. I love you, Mom!

Your daughter,
Janet

Even more than my mom, I have to thank my heavenly Father for His guidance and love throughout this journey. If not for Him and the everyday presence of His Holy Spirit, I could not have relived this time in my life and been able to write this book. He has rescued me from self-destruction and placed me where I am today. My life would be nothing without Him.

I need to thank my wonderful husband for his patience and love. Without his support, I could never have found the courage I needed to make this book a reality. The same also goes for my awesome son, Christopher, for his encouragement and faith in me. During this process, I was not always available when they needed me or patient when interrupted. They sacrificed for me to have this time, but they knew the importance of what I was doing and the effects I pray it will have for others. I love you both!

Thank you to my wonderful daughter, Misty, without whom a lot of my blessings would not be here today. She was the first true blessing that God gave me, though at the time I did not see it that way. I am proud of the young woman she has become. My three grandsons (Zach, Logan, and Trey) would not be a part of my life if it were not for her.

I need to thank my siblings for their unconditional love and support. Though we do not always agree, we always manage to be there for one another. It is a constant source of joy that each of you bring into my life.

A big thank you again to my son and to my nephew, Sam, for their assistance with putting this book together. I stretched my son's patience as much as possible in the process of formatting and working with technology to get this book up and loaded. Sam, bless his heart, had to come in and take over before my son and I choked each other. They have both been critical to the book ever getting out for others to read. I love you both dearly!

Last but not least, I am thankful I was terminated from my job in 2012 though it was without cause. SERIOUSLY, I am indebted to this upheaval in my life! This episode was just another example of God making a way when we see no way. This situation was meant for my harm, but God turned it around for my good. At the time this occurred, I was deeply hurt and disillusioned but as always, God was faithful. When He steered me towards writing this book, I constantly complained I had no time. Well, guess what ... He gave me the time I needed. He allowed me to be terminated which gave me all the time possible. It brings to my mind the story of Joseph in the Bible. Though this incident was in no way as traumatic as Joseph's, it reminds me of Genesis 50:20 that states, *"But as for you, you meant evil against me; but God meant it for good, in order to bring it about as it is this day, to save many people."* I know God has a purpose for this book, and it will touch the lives He is directing it towards. The saving of one life is what it is all about. This trial in my life allowed my faith to grow tremendously and provided the time I needed to complete this task which the Lord had been nudging me to do for years. Just another testimony of God knowing the end from the beginning. (Revelation 22:13, *"I am the Alpha and the Omega, the Beginning and the End, the First and the Last."*)

God's leading me to write this book and my reluctance to do so is another prime example that when God wants you to do something and you ignore Him, He will make a way for it to be done. Sometimes this is good for us, as was the case here, but at other times, it is not. Learn right away to discern God's voice. It is life changing and will make all the difference in your journey on this earth. (John 10:4, "*And when He brings out His own sheep, He goes before them; and the sheep follow Him, for they know His voice.*")

As I shared earlier, I had an opportunity not long ago to become somewhat involved with The Pregnancy Center. I went through counseling to become a mentor of sorts to those who come to the center seeking answers and looking for help. Support your local Pregnancy Center. It is a way to give back for all they do for others. Because of them, I grew so much more determined to share my story. I am here should you need to talk.

I would love to hear from you with comments about my book, with prayer requests, or simply to say hello! You may contact me at janet_nicholson@aol.com.

Please ask to be signed up to receive notice when my next book, entitled "The Battles Within" is released in early 2019.

God Bless,
Janet Molton Nicholson

Junior Prom – 1974

In Donnie's Mother's kitchen during his 1st Military Leave – Latter 1974

In Donnie's Mother's kitchen again 36 years later!

Our long awaited wedding day... you can see how emotions took over!

Finally, let me introduce Mr. and Mrs. Donald Lee Nicholson.